CONTENTS

ACKNOWLEDGMENTS

I WISH TO ACKNOWLEDGE the invaluable guidance of my literary agent, Greg Johnson, in the early stages of this book's development.

I also wish to thank Brian Smith, my editor, for his careful review of the manuscript and his thoughtful suggestions on improving it.

Thanks to Baker Publishing for believing in me and giving me the opportunity to tell these stories for generations yet to come. And thanks to Rebekah Guzman, Amy Ballor, and the rest of the Baker Books team for their patience in granting me an extended deadline. I trust they feel that the extra time has been worth it!

Finally, a very special thank-you to my wife, Cheryl Krusen, for her unflagging support every step along the way. Love to you all!

INTRODUCTION

I WAS TWENTY-NINE YEARS OLD when I became a Christ follower. It didn't happen overnight. Early in the process, when I was reading the Bible on my own, a co-worker asked me if I was "born again." I stared at him blankly. I had no idea what he was talking about. No one had ever spoken to me before about the need to be "born again."

Looking back over my life, I certainly had many blessings, including a godly grandmother who inspired in me a sincere devotion to God. But her influence over me waned following her death when I was eleven years old. By my midteen years I believed in a vague sort of agnosticism that hardened into dark nihilism by my early twenties.

Then I traveled to Australia for a writing assignment and read the Bible as part of my research. Until that time I had wanted to be a big-shot director and writer in Hollywood—rich and successful with a woman or two on each arm. But as

I read the Bible, I began turning from a world I could see to one I could not see. I began a conscious search for truth—if truth could be found—and fell in love with a man I encountered in the pages of the Bible. The romance lasted nearly two years until I finally succumbed wholly to his beauty and gave him my all. I'll never forget the first thought that went through my mind when I made that sweet surrender to Jesus Christ: *I'll never be a filmmaker now.*

My assumption, of course, was that wholehearted faith in Christ and commitment to the Gospels would translate into a life of ministry as the ultimate outlet for self-expression and service to God. Naturally enough, I began to wonder if I might become a pastor or a missionary to some far-off land. I did, in fact, become a missionary for two years, but in time, I came to understand that service to God has manifold, indeed unlimited, expressions. In truth, if God exists, then one should expect to find those who love him in every field of human endeavor.

The twelve individuals I have gotten to know through writing this book have become personal friends. They are highly regarded today for their contributions to science and medicine, literature and philanthropy, government and diplomacy. Unfortunately, people seldom—if ever—remember them for the rich storehouses of faith that gave their lives meaning and purpose in the first place.

It's time to change that. It's time to let the record show that *They Were Christians.*

While writing this book, I found myself crying out at times to the "ghosts" of Abraham, Dag, Frederick, and the others, saying, "We'll make this part of your story known!"

I was repeatedly moved to tears as I considered how much the living God had been so much a part of their lives.

But please understand. These are not exhaustive biographies. Rather, they are more akin to profiles on what Paul Harvey might have called "the rest of the story," specifically those Christian elements in the lives of twelve people who changed the world for the better. May their examples inspire and encourage you, as they have me, and may we all let our light so shine before others that the world will see our good deeds and glorify our Father in heaven (Matt. 5:16).

DAG HAMMARSKJÖLD

I remember Dag Hammarskjöld's clear blue eyes as
much as anything else about him. I also recall my child's
sense that he was a good man, a kind man. I was nine
years old when his plane went down under mysterious
circumstances in what is today the African nation of
Zambia. *How terribly sad!* I thought. He had been on a
peacekeeping mission for the United Nations, and it had
cost him his life.

I discerned a different reaction to Dag's death from
most of the adults in my world. Dag Hammarskjöld had
been secretary-general of the United Nations, and to
them the UN was a suspect organization, dangerously
left-leaning. Some would have called it diabolical. The
furthest thing from anyone's mind was that the UN
might have been led by a person of sincere Christian
faith. And yet it was. Unmistakably so, as was revealed
in 1963 when Dag's private journal was published

posthumously—originally in Swedish, and a year later in English under the title *Markings*.

Twenty years after Dag's death I found myself in his native Sweden facing a crossroads in my life. For several years I had been on a quest for spiritual truth, a self-styled search that had led me to study Hinduism, Buddhism, Taoism, Islam, and finally Christianity. By that time I had read the Bible cover to cover and had concluded that the way to God is through Christ. But how does one enter Christ? For someone like me, who grew up largely outside the church, it was a mystery. All I could do was continue to read the Bible and seek the truth as best I could.

Then one fine October morning as I sat alongside the Motala River in Norrköping, Jesus's words from the Gospel of Matthew came forcefully to mind: "Unless you are converted and become as little children, you will by no means enter the kingdom of heaven" (Matt. 18:3 NKJV).

Suddenly, I began to cry. I felt like a lost child who had been transported miraculously home. All that was left for me to do was walk up to the door, open it, and enter in. When I stood up from that riverbank, I was a new creation in Christ.

I made no connection to Dag Hammarskjöld at the time—that would come later. But as I consider his life and legacy now, I realize that one of the greatest statesmen of the twentieth century (indeed, of any century) had been my brother in the Christian faith. He left me—and the world—a shining example of what it means to serve others "and so fulfill the law of Christ" (Gal. 6:2 NKJV).

PER LIND'S HEART WAS HEAVY. And how could it not be? He looked out the window of the Boeing 707, staring at the billowing clouds that appeared to float slowly past. The scene was worthy of a painting, or at least a photograph. Per knew he would produce neither one. He had made this trip many times before.

He touched the side pocket of his jacket, instinctively feeling the shape of the letter that had arrived less than two weeks ago. It had been mailed to him by Dag from Stockholm, asking him to take charge of his papers and personal belongings in New York should there be a need. Should anything happen to him . . .

Per felt a lump in his throat.

During the first three years of Dag's tenure as secretary-general, Per had served as his personal assistant and had continued to stay in close contact. He and his wife and children had become like family to the brilliant, soft-spoken diplomat, who had no wife or children of his own.

And now the unthinkable.

There was no fanfare when Per's plane landed at Idlewild Airport in New York City. No news reporters, no photographers as there had been in 1953 when he and Dag had landed at the same airport and Dag had given his first interview to the press corps. This was just another early autumn day in "the city that never sleeps."

Per was soon at work on the thirty-eighth floor of the UN Secretariat Building enlisting the help of Dag's personal secretary, Hannah Platz, and other staff members. Everyone maintained a professional attitude, which made Per's job easier and helped the time pass. They spoke in soft, solemn tones while sorting through Dag's extensive papers, as though the former secretary-general were himself nearby, taking a nap, perhaps, and not to be disturbed.

No, that's not quite the analogy, Per thought. Dag was known for near superhuman stamina, working eighteen and twenty hours a day for weeks on end.

Per detected a chill and noticed that Dag's office window was cracked open. Dag had liked it that way, especially in the summer when he would open the window wider to hear the sounds of the tugboat horns and ferry whistles out on the East River. As if on cue, a tugboat released a powerful blast, and Per felt the window shake slightly in his hand. He closed it.

After sorting out Dag's affairs at the UN, Per made the trip to the weekend home Dag had rented in Brewster, New York, sixty miles north of the city. And then the final stop—Dag's residence on East 73rd Street near Park Avenue.

The apartment was just as Per had remembered. It occupied two floors and was furnished sparingly yet beautifully. A grand dining room, a living room, and a library with numerous rare books made up the ground floor. This was where Dag liked to spend much of his free time. Fluent in four languages, he was a bibliophile who enjoyed translating plays and poetry. Per recalled with a smile the dozens of offers that had poured in during those early days. Dag was constantly receiving invitations to one upper-crust New York social function after another, most of which Per was instructed to decline politely, as the secretary-general preferred entertaining in small groups, often just a guest or two, at his apartment home.

Per entered the library, his eyes settling on the empty fireplace, above which hung a mountain hiker's pick. He smiled grimly. Dag had been an avid outdoorsman and mountain climber throughout his life, and the ice pick was a gift from the Sherpa mountaineer, Tenzing Norgay. In 1953, Tenzing and Sir Edmund Hillary were the first men to scale Mt. Everest. Underneath the pick was an inscription from Tenzing that read: "So you may climb to even greater heights."

Per ascended the staircase and entered Dag's bedroom. He made his way to the window and looked at the street below. This was the view Dag had enjoyed every day. What was he thinking about before he left New York that last time? Before he boarded the plane to the world's newest trouble spot—the former Belgian Congo? Some were saying he had experienced a premonition of his death. Per was doubtful of that. It had been his secretary, Hannah, who had advised him to put his affairs in order before that last fateful trip to Africa.

Per looked slowly around the well-kept room and sighed. *So quiet. So still. What lonely hours Dag must have spent here.* Per sat on the edge of the bed. A Bible lay on top of the nightstand. Per had not known Dag to be particularly religious, though he had known and admired him as a person of unshakeable integrity. He absentmindedly opened the nightstand drawer. Inside was a buff-colored folder, well worn with age, containing what appeared to be some sort of manuscript. A United Nations secretariat envelope bearing the typewritten name "Leif Belfrage" was clipped to the outside of the folder, and on the envelope's lower left-hand corner was a handwritten word in Swedish—*Personligt* ("Personal").

Per sensed immediately that the folder contained something important—perhaps a political diary—but that was not for him to speculate about. Leif Belfrage, Sweden's permanent undersecretary of foreign affairs, was Dag's close friend and Per's friend as well. Per would personally see that the folder and sealed envelope were taken to Stockholm and handed over to Dr. Belfrage.

Per stood up. There was much more work to do.

Dr. Belfrage removed his reading glasses and carefully set Dag's letter to one side. In the letter, Dag referred to the attached folder and the diary it contained, inviting his friend to publish the entries "if you find them worth publishing." Dag described his journal "as a sort of white book concerning my negotiations with myself—and with God."[1]

"A sort of white book," Leif repeated to himself. Dag was using the diplomatic term for an official government report, a position paper bound in white. Leif looked out his office window. Freezing rain was splattering against the pane, seemingly trying to get his attention. *Negotiations with himself—and with God.* Now, this was surprising. He did not know Dag to be a regular churchgoer. He looked again at the folder, fingering its edges. He did recall—albeit dimly— that Dag had mentioned something once about keeping a diary. That alone was not unusual, of course, especially for one as fastidious in his work habits as Dag. What made this document so compelling was the identity of its author, the many world figures he had known, and his sudden, untimely death. Without exactly framing the question as such, Leif had to wonder what behind-the-scenes maneuvering, political exposé, or scandal such a diary might contain.

He opened the folder. Centered on the manuscript's cover page was a single word in Swedish: *Vägmärken* ("Markings"). *A curious title,* Dr. Belfrage mused, wondering if it had some connection with Dag's love of the outdoors and the trail marks hikers leave behind to find their way home. He thumbed through the ream of paper and took a cursory look. The diary contained nearly two hundred typewritten pages, some containing just a few lines, beginning with the year 1925 (when Dag was twenty years old) and ending on August 24, 1961—three weeks before his death.

Dr. Belfrage couldn't help himself. He took a peek at the UN years.

Dag Hjalmar Agne Carl Hammarskjöld was the youngest of four children born into an aristocratic family that had served the kings and queens of Sweden since the seventeenth century. His father, Hjalmar Hammarskjöld, had been prime minister of Sweden during the First World War, steering the country on a neutral course, while his three older brothers were likewise prominent Swedes: Bo, a diplomat; Ake, a judge on the International Court of Justice; and Sten, a journalist and novelist.

By all accounts, Dag was the brightest of them all—an internationally recognized economist fluent in Swedish, French, English, and German. His highly accomplished father once said, "If I were half as smart as Dag, I might have done something in life." Dag served as secretary and, later, governor of the central bank of Sweden, cabinet secretary in the Ministry of Foreign Affairs, and a delegate to the Paris conference that established the Marshall Plan. In 1951, he became vice chairman of the Swedish delegation to the United Nations General Assembly in Paris, and a year later of the Swedish delegation to the General Assembly in New York.

Despite his accomplishments and abilities, Dag's nomination to the secretary-generalship of the UN came as a complete surprise—especially to him! When friends first told him the news in Stockholm on April 1, 1953, he thought it was an April Fools' Day joke.

The Security Council had been meeting for weeks in New York trying in vain to agree on who would take the place of Norway's Trygve Lie, the first secretary-general, who had resigned in November the previous year. The Cold War was in full swing at the time, and the superpowers disagreed on seemingly every issue, including who would lead the United Nations. An acrimonious debate showed no signs of letting up until finally a compromise was reached with the nomination of Dag Hammarskjöld. Dag, who was considered a competent technocrat without obvious political leanings, seemed a safe bet not to rock the boat.

A hurriedly written cablegram from the Security Council dispelled the notion of an April Fools' Day joke. It read, "In view of the immense importance of this post, especially at the present time, members of the Security Council express the earnest hope that you will agree to accept the appointment if, as they hope and believe, it is shortly made by the General Assembly."[2]

Dag told them he needed to sleep on it.

Two days passed before he cabled the Security Council with his answer. After admitting to "strong feelings of personal insufficiency," he nonetheless concluded that he "could not refuse to accept the task imposed upon [him]." What the world did not know—indeed, what most of his friends did not know—was that Dag, always an intensely private individual, had prayed years before for God to give him a life-defining task.

Confiding privately in his journal at the time of the nomination, he wrote, "When the hour strikes, He takes what is His. What have you to say? Your prayer has been answered, as you know. God has a use for you, even though what He asks doesn't happen to suit you at the moment."[3]

And then a day or two later—the date is not certain—he penned this brief entry: "Not I, but God in me."[4]

On April 7, 1953, the General Assembly approved the Security Council's nomination and elected Dag Hammarskjöld secretary-general of the UN. He was forty-seven years old.

As Dag prepared to fly to the United States with Per Lind, his newly appointed personal assistant, he wrote this in his journal: "I am the vessel. The draught is God's. And God is the thirsty one."[5]

As Dag exited the plane at Idlewild Airport on April 9, the stocky and forthright Mr. Lie welcomed his successor to "the most impossible job in the world." In a prepared statement to the press, Dag acknowledged that in his new role, "The private man should disappear and the international public servant take his place. The public servant is there in order to assist . . . those who make the decisions which frame history . . . He is active as an instrument, a catalyst, perhaps an inspirer—he serves."[6] In Dag's case, such a "servant" was also called to follow in the steps of Christ. As he wrote in his journal at the time, "He who has surrendered himself to it knows that the Way ends on the cross—even when it is leading him through the jubilation of Gennesaret or the triumphal entry into Jerusalem."[7]

The day after he arrived in New York, Dag took the oath of office in the cavernous General Assembly Hall of the United Nations building and then made personal remarks to the representatives from the sixty member states. "I am here to serve you all," he said simply. In a reference to Easter, celebrated five days earlier, he added, "May I remind you of the great memory just celebrated by the Christian world? May I do so because of what that memory tells us of the redeeming power of true dedication to peace and goodwill towards men?" Then, looking into the sea of faces representing the nations of Earth, he said, "We are of different creeds and convictions . . . But common to us all, and above all other convictions, stands the truth once expressed by a Swedish poet when he said that the greatest prayer of man does not ask for victory but for peace."[8]

First impressions of the new secretary-general were favorable. Dag initiated a review of every aspect of UN operations and procedures, taking time to meet with each staff member personally—a task that took many weeks to complete. He established a secretariat of nearly four thousand administrators and drafted new regulations defining their responsibilities. He also found ways to trim the budget. Dag hoped to create not only a well-oiled machine but also a community of like-minded souls, men and women who would work tirelessly for peace on earth and goodwill toward all.

As to his personal beliefs, Dag spoke openly later that year in a radio interview with broadcast journalist Edward R. Murrow.

From generations of soldiers and government officials on my father's side I inherited a belief that no life was more satisfactory than one of selfless service to your country—or humanity. This service required a sacrifice of all personal interests, but likewise the courage to stand up unflinchingly for your convictions. From scholars and clergymen on my mother's side, I inherited a belief that, in the very radical sense of the Gospels, all men were equals as children of God, and should be met and treated by us as our masters in God.[9]

One of Dag's earliest initiatives in the political arena took place in 1954 when he offered to help ease tensions between Israel and Jordan in a dispute over water rights. Though his efforts did not directly resolve the conflict, world leaders began to take note that the new secretary-general was serious about building bridges between disparate groups and nations. The UN, with its lofty ideals and aims, was taking on a human face.

It was decidedly that human touch that Dag utilized at the end of the year when he traveled to mainland China (not yet a member of the UN) to seek the release of fifteen US airmen who had been taken prisoner during the Korean War. It was a foregone conclusion that the Chinese government would not recognize Dag's authority as secretary-general of the UN. But a personal appeal was a different matter. China had expressed its willingness to subscribe to the Charter of the United Nations, and Dag encouraged their acceptance into the world body despite strenuous objections from the United States. "If you want to negotiate with somebody," he once remarked with humor, "it is rather useful to have them at the table."[10]

Dag sent a personal cablegram to Chou En-lai, the Chinese prime minister, expressing his desire to meet with him in Peking for direct discussions. Six days later, Dag received an invitation to come. "I go to Peking because I believe in personal talks," said Dag to the press shortly before departing New York City on December 30, 1954. "I can only say I will do my best."[11]

Either on or close to New Year's Day, a few days before meeting with Chou En-lai, Dag recorded in his journal the following prayer acknowledging he was under God's hand: "And in Thee is all power and goodness. Give me a pure heart that I may see Thee, a humble heart that I may hear Thee, a heart of love that I may serve Thee, a heart of faith that I may abide in Thee."[12]

The talks went well—better than expected. But when Dag returned from China two weeks later, his hands were empty. The Chinese had given him no direct response, and as new crises clamored for Dag's attention, the fate of the US airmen, all of whom had been sentenced to long prison terms, was left in limbo. Dag, however, continued his quiet diplomacy, maintaining personal contact with the Chinese premier. And then on July 29, 1955, while celebrating his fiftieth birthday on a fishing expedition in Sweden, he received news that the US servicemen would be released soon. It was a birthday gift to him from Chou En-lai. Though the Chinese government did not credit Dag's mediation directly, the world knew that the airmen owed their newfound freedom to the soft-spoken Swede who dared to believe in "personal talks."

Later that night, most likely after his fishing companions had all drifted off to sleep, Dag removed from his rucksack a book that had been his constant companion for thirty-five years, *The Imitation of Christ* by Thomas à Kempis. It, too, had been a birthday gift . . . from his devout mother, Agnes. Dag made a brief journal entry that night, quoting à Kempis, who wrote, "Why do you seek rest? You were only created for labor."

Three days later, reacting, one would assume, to the worldwide acclaim he was receiving for his pivotal role in the release of the airmen, Dag confided in his journal, quoting from the psalms. "Surely men of low degree are vanity, and men of high degree are a lie: to be laid in the balance, they are altogether lighter than vanity" (Ps. 62:9).

He also quoted from Psalm 115. "Not unto us, O LORD, but unto thy name give glory" (v. 1).

Dr. Belfrage looked up from the manuscript. The freezing rain had changed to gently falling snow that frosted over the edges of his office windows. *Not a mention yet of anyone by name,* he marveled. Knowing that 1956 had been a watershed year for Dag and the UN, he returned to his reading, wondering if Dag's acute introspection would give way to at least some scrutiny of world events and the major players whom he knew so well.

Indeed, in 1956, Dag experienced the greatest challenges yet to his leadership at the UN. The primary area of contention was the Sinai Peninsula and, more particularly, the Suez Canal, which Britain and France managed jointly. Egypt's president, Gamal Abdel Nasser, openly courted the Soviet

Union, an overture that displeased the Western powers and set the stage for a showdown between East and West. When the World Bank abruptly withdrew support for the construction of the Aswan Dam on the upper Nile, President Nasser retaliated by nationalizing the Suez Canal and imposing taxes on foreign shipping. France and Britain threatened the use of force to reassert their control over the area, while the Soviet Union came out strongly in support of Egypt.

There was talk of a nuclear Armageddon.

Dag labored ceaselessly for months to bring all parties to the bargaining table and appeared to have succeeded when a truce was implemented on October 13. Then two weeks later, French, British, and Israeli forces launched a surprise attack on Egypt and seized the canal area.

Dag felt shocked and betrayed by the invasion, but he knew where his strength lay. He turned again to the psalms. "I will both lay me down in peace, and sleep: for thou, Lord, only makest me dwell in safety" (Ps. 4:8).

And again, "Rest in the Lord . . . fret not thyself because of him who prospereth in his way, because of the man who bringeth wicked devices to pass" (Ps. 37:7, 8).

World public opinion was largely unfavorable to the military incursion in the Sinai, but that did not keep France and Britain, permanent members of the Security Council, from blocking every effort to achieve a peaceful solution to the crisis. Dag made it clear that, under such circumstances, he was willing to resign. A majority of member states, particularly the smaller and newer nations who knew they had a friend in Dag, disagreed. The UN called an emergency session of the General Assembly, and a resolution passed demanding an immediate cease-fire and troop withdrawal from the Suez.

Additionally, a military force was to be formed from ten of the nonaligned nations and sent to the area to keep the peace.

In view of the General Assembly's overwhelming support of Dag's position, Britain and France backed down, and the first soldiers of the United Nations Emergency Force (UNEF) arrived in Egypt in November 1956. The group eventually numbered six thousand soldiers and maintained a cease-fire in the region until all foreign troops had withdrawn from the battle zone by March 1957. UNEF soldiers continued to guard the border for another ten years.

It was a major triumph for Dag, but instead of pointing the finger at others or gloating in his diplomatic success, he reflected, "Hallowed be Thy name, not mine. Thy kingdom come, not mine. Thy will be done, not mine."[13]

On Christmas Eve, he remarked that "your own efforts 'did not bring it to pass,' only God—but rejoice if God found a use for your efforts in His work. Rejoice if you feel that what you did was 'necessary,' but remember, even so, that you were simply the instrument."[14]

Less than a year later, on September 26, 1957, Dag was reelected secretary-general for another five-year term. That same day he wrote in his journal that "the best and most wonderful thing that can happen to you in this life is that you should be silent and let God work and speak."[15]

Such were the private meditations of the man known to millions around the world as "Mr. UN."

He would never finish his second term, of course. In his "negotiations with God" Dag increasingly felt a sense of impending death. It was not an end to be avoided, provided it came in accord with God's will. This entry was among his trail marks, or "markings," during 1957: "Do not seek death. Death will find you. But seek the road which makes death a fulfillment."[16]

In July 1960, a growing political crisis in the newly independent Congo, formerly a Belgian colony, was threatening to mire the superpowers in another Korean War, something almost everyone sought to avoid without knowing exactly how. It was another problem "for Dag to fix," at least behind closed doors, even if publicly he had to endure the grandstanding of world leaders like Nikita Khrushchev, who thumped his fist on his UN desk while demanding Dag's resignation as secretary-general.

Dag's position was secure, of course, as Khrushchev was fully aware. The UN had nearly doubled in size from the time Dag had first assumed the helm, and its member states were overwhelmingly in favor of him staying on. Dag, too, was prepared to stay the course, though for reasons no one surmised.

The fateful moment came shortly after midnight on September 18, 1961, when Dag's UN plane, a DC-6 with sixteen people on board, crashed in the forest roughly seven miles from the runway at Ndola in Northern Rhodesia (now Zambia). Dag had been on his way to hold personal talks with Moïse Tshombe, the leader of the secessionist Congo province of Katanga. To this day, conspiracy theories persist that several of the European powers, possibly joined by the United States, arranged Dag's death in order to protect the fabulous wealth of their Katanga mineral concessions.

Dag had been for peace and they for war.

Dr. Belfrage pushed away the diary and rubbed his eyes. Memories of Dag's funeral ceremony came vividly to mind.

An estimated 250,000 mourners gathered in Stockholm for a torchlight procession, after which Dag's casket was transported north to the university town of Uppsala where he had grown up.

Heads of state from around the world assembled to pay their last respects.

Six pallbearers in top hats and long black coats lowered the flower-covered casket into an open grave.

The resolute voice of Lutheran Archbishop Gunnar Hultgren rang through the air. "Sleep you now in the garden of heaven. Rest in peace, Dag Hammarskjöld."

When the funeral ended, church bells rang from Malmo in the south of Sweden to Malmberget in the north, followed by an hour of silence throughout the nation.[17]

Dr. Belfrage walked over to his window. As far as the eye could see, the ground was covered in freshly fallen snow, pure and white. It seemed a fitting backdrop to the autobiographical "profile" of his friend, Dag Hammarskjöld. Not one word of opprobrium, not one word of complaint or bitterness toward others. No mention of names, no secrets divulged. Just the frank and unflattering self-examination of a man who had sought God's purpose in life and was willing to walk the road that fate had marked out for him.

And in that moment, Dr. Belfrage knew, beyond the shadow of a doubt, that Dag's "white book" concerning his "negotiations with [himself] and with God" was, indeed, "worthy to be published."

At the time of his death, Dag had intended to stay only a day or two in Katanga and, consequently, had left most of his travel belongings behind in the capital city of Léopoldville. On the bedside table where he had spent his last night was his copy of *The Imitation of Christ*. Inside was a bookmark—a plain card on which he had written his oath of office as secretary-general of the UN. The passage marked in the book was the following reflection on self-denial and an acceptance of God's will:

> Lord, provided that my will remain true and firm towards Thee, do with me whatsoever it shall please Thee to do. For it cannot but be good, whatever Thou shalt do with me. If Thou wilt have me to be in darkness, be Thou blessed; and if Thou wilt have me to be in light, be Thou again blessed; if Thou vouchsafe to comfort me, be Thou blessed; and if it be Thy will I should be afflicted, be Thou still equally blessed . . . Keep me from all sin, and I will fear neither death nor hell.[18]

The analogy is, to me, inescapable: Dag's secular and spiritual identities were closely intertwined and clearly complemented one another. Or as Dag wrote in his diary, "In our era, the road to holiness necessarily passes through the world of action."[19]

On December 10, 1961, Dag Hammarskjöld was posthumously awarded the Nobel Peace Prize. President John F. Kennedy called him the "greatest statesman of our century." Now I know what I didn't know then. Dag Hammarskjöld had been the greatest among us because he had been the least and the servant of all (see Matt. 20:26; Luke 9:48).

FREDERICK DOUGLASS[1]

Many life changes occur gradually, over time. But I can attest to the fact that change can also be the result of one gut-wrenching experience—a watershed moment in life.

In the spring of 1973, I was a twenty-year-old student majoring in radio, TV, and film who had transferred from Harvard University to the University of Texas at Austin. I hadn't been interested in, or even loosely involved with, religious activities since my early teens. For me, God had become someone—or something—too far away to capture my attention.

In April that year, my eighteen-year-old girlfriend from New York came to stay with me for a week.

Yes, the hippie era was alive and well.

Our last day together was going to be Easter Sunday, and I somehow got the idea that we should go to church that day. A handsome church sat right across the street from the residence hall in which I lived, and I suggested to Elizabeth, my girlfriend, that we go there for Easter service. She was fine with the idea.

That Sunday morning we put on our best clothes and made the short walk over to the church. I could hear organ music coming from inside the historic building, and I squeezed Elizabeth's hand tighter. It was going to be a beautiful day. I tend to run late for appointments, so I had made sure we'd arrived in plenty of time for the service. Ahead of us I could see other people walking up the stone steps and entering the church. All was well.

And then, just as we reached the top of the stairs and were about to enter the sanctuary, a pale, middle-aged church usher with slicked-back hair emerged from the shadows and blocked our path. I'll never forget the look in his eyes. He seemed both fearful and hateful at the same time.

"There's no more room inside," he said, barring our way.

"No more room?" I asked. "What do you mean?"

"There's no more room. The service is full."

Elizabeth was ready to turn and leave. I was not. I knew the man was lying. Another couple passed us from behind and entered the church. The usher said nothing. He just stood there unflinching, working his jaw around as though chewing on a bone. Anger and resentment rose inside me.

You see, Elizabeth and I were an interracial couple, and while the two of us being together would hardly raise eyebrows nowadays, back then it was uncommon in the South. Texas laws against miscegenation had been ruled unconstitutional only six years prior to us dating. Not that man's laws were of much concern to the two of us. Our love was growing stronger every day and our relationship becoming more and more serious.

But one thing gave me pause. My family had rejected her (and by extension me), and her family was fractured and dysfunctional. Elizabeth and I were on our own. I remember thinking at the time that perhaps it was God who was absent in our lives. That we needed his presence to fill the gap left by a missing family and to ease the awful isolation we sometimes felt.

In the end we made no scene on the church steps. We turned and walked back to the residence hall.

That one experience in Austin changed the course of my life. I began using it as justification for passing judgment on all Christians. My theory about needing God in my life might still be relevant, but from that day forward I ruled out ever finding him in the Christian religion.

The sting of rejection I felt, however, hardly compares to the injuries and insults suffered by the subject of our next biography. By virtue of being a slave in the antebellum South, society viewed Frederick Douglass as intrinsically less than human. Despite the tortuous attempts theologians made at the time to justify involuntary servitude, they could not ultimately avoid the reality that slavery was ungodly and unloving. Frederick Douglass's human potential made no difference to them. He was born a slave and deemed a piece of property akin to a farm animal.

Needless to say, he did not view himself this way. From the time he was a child, he had wished to be free. He wanted to find his place in the sun and the chance to fulfill his God-given potential. He faced a lifelong struggle—not only to be free himself but also for his fellow slaves to be free. Historians commend him for his towering intellect and bravery, but very few acknowledge the vibrant faith that sustained him and provided the moral compass he needed to stay the course and finish the race that began so inconspicuously at his birth on Maryland's Eastern Shore in 1818.

"LOOK ME IN THE EYE. DON'T BE AFRAID."

Her voice was kind and sincere, and nine-year-old Freddy was finally beginning to believe that it was indeed safe to look Miss Sophia, wife of his new master, Hugh Auld, in the eye.

He had come to the Auld home in Baltimore a few months before. He was a gift of sorts from Hugh Auld's brother, Thomas, and his wife, Lucretia. It was a welcome change of scenery for the young slave.

He had already seen more in his few years living in Talbot County, Maryland, than any child should—arbitrary and brutal whippings, children forcibly separated from their mothers, unprosecuted cold-blooded murders. He had suffered from hunger and cold all his life. He had never owned a pair of trousers or shoes and slept on a mud floor at night. But at least he had not been whipped or shot. Not yet anyway.

While serving the Aulds, Freddy was to do chores and run errands for the missus while also functioning as a companion for their son, Tommy. Mr. Auld, a busy shipbuilder, could hardly be bothered with keeping track of the young slave and left Sophia to manage him entirely.

"Miss Sophy" had a magnanimous nature. She had supported herself as a workingwoman before marrying Hugh and lacked the common attitude held at that time toward slaves. She simply regarded Freddy as she would any other child—a boy in need of love and care—and he flowered under her tutelage. "How could I hang down my head, and speak with bated breath," Frederick wrote in his autobiography years later, "when there was no pride to scorn me, no coldness to repel me, and no hatred to inspire me with fear? I therefore soon learned to regard her as something more akin to a mother than a slaveholding mistress . . . I was human, and she, dear lady, knew and felt me to be so."

Miss Sophy was also very devout. During the day, while her husband was at work, Freddy often observed her singing hymns, praying, and reading the Bible aloud.

"The frequent hearing of my mistress reading the Bible soon awakened my curiosity in respect to this mystery of reading, and roused in me the desire to learn. Having no fear of my kind mistress (she had then given me no reason to fear), I frankly asked her to teach me to read; and, without hesitation, the dear woman began the task, and very soon, by her assistance, I was master of the alphabet, and could spell words of three or four letters."

Miss Sophy was delighted by her pupil's development and shared the news with her husband. "My mistress seemed almost as proud of my progress as if I had been her own child; and, supposing that her husband would be as well pleased, she made no secret of what she was doing for me."

Hugh Auld, however, did not share his wife's excitement in the least. Apart from the fact that it was illegal to teach a slave to read, there were the inevitable and undesirable consequences should Freddy actually gain an education.

"If you teach this boy how to read the Bible," Hugh Auld informed his wife, "there'll be no keeping him. It'll forever unfit him for the duties of a slave. Why, he'll then want to know how to write; and, this accomplished, he'll be running away with himself!"

Mr. Auld forbade his wife to ever teach Freddy again and considered the matter settled. It was not. "Master Hugh's discourse was the first decidedly antislavery lecture to which it had been my lot to listen," wrote Frederick. "His iron sentences—cold and harsh—awakened within me a slumbering train of vital thought . . . Wise as Mr. Auld was, he evidently underrated my comprehension . . . That which he most loved I most hated; and the very determination which he expressed to keep me in ignorance, only rendered me the more resolute in seeking intelligence. In learning to read, therefore, I am not sure that I do not owe quite as much to the opposition of my master as to the kindly assistance of my amiable mistress."

Nonetheless, Hugh Auld's pernicious words had found their mark—not in Freddy but in Miss Sophy. As a good wife endeavoring to obey her husband in all things, Miss Sophy now sought to put Freddy in his "proper place" by forbidding him to read and punishing him if he disobeyed. She could not, however, totally isolate her young charge, nor quench his thirst for knowledge. Freddy continued an education of sorts among the white boys in the neighborhood with whom he mingled and played. He usually kept hidden with him a copy of Noah Webster's spelling book, and when he was sent on an errand or during his allotted playtime, he would take out the primer and ask his fellows on the street to give him a lesson. They were usually eager to oblige.

"For a single biscuit, any of my hungry little comrades would give me a lesson more valuable to me than bread. Not every one, however, demanded this consideration, for there were those who took pleasure in teaching me whenever I had a chance to be taught by them."

As the years passed, Frederick took advantage of every opportunity to build his vocabulary and increase his knowledge. He surreptitiously borrowed Master Tommy's school notebooks, especially the copying books used to teach children how to write, and through hard work and patience taught himself the art of writing. He also continued to read everything he could find. He learned of the abolitionist movement by reading *The Columbian Orator* and by weighing the many compelling arguments against slavery that were presented in public debates.

He also maintained a keen interest in the Bible. He recounts in his autobiography how he lovingly rescued torn fragments of the Bible from the gutters of Baltimore streets, washing and drying the pages so that he "might get a word or two of wisdom from them."

Around the age of thirteen, Frederick began to feel a "need of God as a father and protector." He heard the gospel preached by a white Methodist minister named Hanson who "thought that all men, great and small, bond and free, were sinners in the sight of God; and that they must repent of their sins and be reconciled to God through Christ. I cannot say that I had a very distinct notion of what was required of me; but one thing I knew very well—I was wretched, and had no means of making myself otherwise. Moreover, I knew that I could pray for light."

After several weeks of intense soul-searching and prayer, Frederick "found that change of heart which comes by 'casting all one's care' upon God, and by having faith in Jesus Christ as the Redeemer, Friend, and Savior of those who diligently seek Him."

After his conversion experience, Frederick began to see the world in a new light. "I seemed to live in a new world, surrounded by new objects and animated by new hopes and desires. I loved all mankind—slaveholders not excepted—though I abhorred slavery more than ever. My great concern was, now, to have the world converted. The desire for knowledge increased, and especially did I want a thorough acquaintance with the contents of the Bible."

The young man yearned for a spiritual mentor, and his prayers were answered in the form of a free, elderly black man named Charles Lawson. "His life was a life of prayer," Frederick wrote, "and his words (when he spoke to his friends) were about a better world." Frederick became deeply attached to "Father" or "Uncle" Lawson and regularly went with him to midweek prayer meetings and Sunday services. "The old man could read a little, and I was a great help to him in making out the hard words, for I was a better reader than he. I could teach him 'the letter,' but he could teach me 'the spirit;' and high, refreshing times we had together, in singing, praying and glorifying God . . . Uncle Lawson was my spiritual father and I loved him intensely, and was at his house every chance I got."

Notwithstanding Master Hugh's threats to whip Frederick should he continue associating with Uncle Lawson, Frederick spent as much time as possible with the elderly man. One day the two of them had a conversation that fundamentally altered the course of Frederick's life. Uncle Lawson told his young disciple that the Lord had shown him there was a great work for Frederick to do and that he must prepare for it. He would one day preach the gospel to the entire world.

"But how can that be?" asked Frederick.

"Trust in the Lord," Uncle Lawson said kindly. "He'll bring it to pass in his own good time."

"But, Uncle, don't you see? I'm a slave. A slave for life."

The old man reached out and touched Frederick on the shoulder. "The Lord can make you free, my dear. All things are possible with him. You only need two things." The old man held up his finger. "Have faith in God, Frederick."

Frederick showed no reaction. "And the other?"

"Ask and it shall be given you," said Uncle Lawson, smiling. "If you want liberty, child, then ask for it in faith, and the Lord will give it to you."

Even though Hugh Auld knew that Frederick continued to spend time with Uncle Lawson every chance he got, he never made good on his threats to punish him. It was a sign of sorts to the young man, who now worked and prayed with a lighter heart than before, convinced a wisdom higher than his own was guiding his future and that God would deliver him from bondage.

But it would not happen overnight.

In fact, about three years later Frederick's life took a decided turn for the worse. The kindhearted Lucretia Auld—Hugh and Sophia's sister-in-law who had originally gifted Frederick to them—died, and ownership of Frederick passed to her widowed husband, Thomas. Thomas now obliged his brother, Hugh, to return Frederick to their plantation at St. Michaels.

Upon his return, Frederick's first impressions of the place and its inhabitants were not at all favorable. Thomas had remarried, and whereas Frederick had always considered him a selfish man, his new wife, Rowena, was downright cruel. The slaves at St. Michaels were kept on starvation rations and often resorted to stealing food to survive.

Frederick, now sixteen, regretted that he had not acted on previous impulses to flee the Auld household in Baltimore for freedom in the north. He now realized—too late—that his chances for escape from the backwaters of St. Michaels were unlikely, given its physical isolation from a major city or seaport.

Then in August 1833, about six months after Frederick arrived at St. Michaels, Master Thomas made an unexpected "profession of religion" at a Methodist camp meeting held in the neighboring Bay Side. Thomas was a wealthy and influential man in the area and had previously evinced no great interest in religious affairs, so his "conversion" created quite a stir. Ministers and churchgoers in the region were ecstatic.

Frederick, however, adopted a wait-and-see attitude.

"If he has got religion," Frederick wrote, "he will emancipate his slaves; and if he should not do so much as this, he will at any rate behave toward us more kindly and feed us more generously than he has heretofore done."

Frederick's wishes were doomed on both counts. Master Thomas's conversion may have changed his attitude toward God, but it did nothing to alter his behavior toward his fellow man. Nonetheless, Frederick held out hope. "I was bound to do this in charity for I, too, was religious and had been in the church full three years."

Sadly, there would be no bridging the divide. Frederick longed with every fiber of his being to be free and to make a difference in the world. Hadn't that been the word of prophecy Father Lawson had spoken to him? Thomas Auld, however, enjoyed all the rights and privileges of the slave-owning class, and his interests were focused on maintaining the status quo. He kept an increasingly wary eye on this intelligent, young black man who carried himself with such intrinsic dignity.

Not many months later, Frederick was asked to help teach a Sunday school class for blacks at the house of a free black man in St. Michaels. He warmed to the idea immediately. "Here, thought I, is something worth living for; here is an excellent chance for usefulness; and I shall soon have a company of young friends, lovers of knowledge, like some of my Baltimore friends, from whom I now felt parted forever."

The organizer of the Sunday school, a young white man named Wilson, rounded up several old spelling books and Bibles for the class of twenty students, and Frederick soon became involved in a "good work, simply teaching a few colored children how to read the gospel of the Son of God."

But Thomas Auld would have none of it. The following Sunday, presumably after morning prayers, he and a group of Christian slave owners, armed with sticks and clubs, forcibly disbanded the school and warned Frederick and his students never to meet again for such purposes.

However, that was not the end of the matter.

A few months later, Frederick, deemed increasingly incorrigible by his masters, was designated "to be broken." It was common practice at the time to make slaves more tractable by methodically breaking their will.

Frederick was sent seven miles away to the household of Edward Covey, a hardscrabble tenant farmer with a stellar reputation as the best in the area at "breaking young negroes." Under the terms of the agreement, Frederick was to spend a year as Covey's slave. For Frederick it was an experience somewhere between purgatory and hell.

During the first six months, he was routinely flogged with a cow skin whip and forced to labor from before sunrise to well into the night. Still a teenager, he found himself on the verge of a complete breakdown—just as his masters had intended. He also found himself on the edge of losing his faith.

"How could I pray?" he wrote later. "Covey could pray—Master Auld could pray—I would fain pray; but doubts (arising partly of my own neglect of the means of grace and partly from the sham religion which everywhere prevailed) cast in my mind a doubt upon all religion, and led me to the conviction that prayers were unavailing and delusive."

After one particularly savage beating during which Covey put a deep gash on his forehead, Frederick escaped to the woods. He ran through forest and field to Master Auld's property at St. Michaels and entreated deliverance. Mr. Auld turned a blind eye. "What would you have me do?" he asked Frederick impatiently. "You belong to Mr. Covey for one year, and you must go back to him, come what will."

A dispirited Frederick hid in the woods for several days before finally returning to Covey's house, expecting the worst. It wasn't long in coming. Early the next morning, while Frederick was in the barn preparing the horses for the day's work, Covey snuck up behind him and tackled him to the ground. Frederick had already made the decision to forcibly resist any physical aggression on Covey's part, and soon the two were engaged in an all-out fight. The sixteen-year-old eventually got the better of the hardened slave driver, and Covey called for his cousin, Hughes, to come and help. After one kick from

Frederick, however, Hughes was sprawled out on the floor and unwilling to reenter the fray. Covey, raising his voice, enjoined several of the slaves standing nearby to help, but none of them lifted a finger in his defense. After Frederick had pinned him down for several hours, Covey finally called it quits. Struggling to his feet, sputtering and swearing, he threatened Frederick with a "much worse beating" should he ever resist again. Frederick couldn't help but smile as the battered Covey fetched his hat from the horse dung and staggered back to his house to lick his wounds in private. If word got out that Frederick had fought back and gotten the better of him in the bargain, Covey's reputation as a "negro breaker" would be ruined.

Needless to say, Covey never again bothered Frederick. Indeed, Frederick's resistance to Covey's barbaric cruelty marked a turning point in his life. "I had been nothing before," he wrote in his autobiography. "I was a man now . . . I had reached the point at which I was not afraid to die. This spirit made me a freeman in fact, while I remained a slave in form."

Frederick finished his final six months with Covey before moving to a new, temporary owner, William Freeland, on January 1, 1835.

Though Mr. Freeland treated his human property more kindly than most slave owners in the area, the fact remained that, under the slaveholding system, Frederick enjoyed no individual rights. It was a condition he refused to accept.

Within weeks after moving to Mr. Freeland's plantation, Frederick formed a new Sunday school class. He and his eager students—forty in all—were more circumspect this time around and kept their activities well hidden from prying eyes. The irony of having to study the Bible in secret was not lost on young Frederick, who wrote, "Let the reader reflect upon the fact that in this Christian country, men and women are hiding from professors of religion in barns, in the woods and fields, in order to learn to read the Holy Bible. Those dear souls, who came to my Sabbath school, came *not* because it was popular or reputable to attend such a place, for they came under the liability of having forty stripes laid on their naked backs."

Teaching Sunday school remained one of Frederick's most cherished memories, but it did not take away his desire for personal freedom. "I had now become altogether too big for my chains. Father Lawson's solemn words of what I ought to be, and might be in the providence of God, had not fallen dead on my soul." So, along with five of his Sunday school students, Frederick began planning a daring escape.

Unfortunately, someone in the group was a traitor, and Frederick and the other four were arrested and thrown in jail. Frederick's greatest fear was that he would now be sold to a buyer in the Deep South, from which escape was all but impossible.

Then something unexpected happened. Thomas Auld turned down several attractive offers to sell Frederick and decided to send him back to Baltimore. Auld told Frederick that he wanted him to learn a trade and that, if he behaved himself, he would be set free at the age of twenty-five. "The promise had but one fault," Frederick remarked later. "It seemed too good to be true."

Back again in Baltimore, Frederick learned to be a ship caulker and began earning good money. But at the end of each week he was obligated to turn over all his earnings to Master Hugh. Before long, he was again planning an escape.

There would be no betrayals this time. Frederick had fallen in love with a free black woman in Baltimore named Anna Murray, who was five years his senior. Anna was a laundress, and she used money from her savings to secure Frederick a sailor's uniform and identity papers attesting to his status as a freeman. On September 3, 1838, he boarded a train east of Baltimore Harbor and headed north. From Havre de Grace, Maryland, Frederick crossed the Susquehanna River by steam ferry, then continued by train and steamboat to Philadelphia and finally New York City, where he was welcomed into the home of David Ruggles, a printer and well-known abolitionist. The entire journey had taken less than twenty-four hours.

Anna joined him in New York shortly thereafter, and the two were married. But they were not out of danger. At that time, bounty hunters roamed the streets of New York City, and even free blacks ran the risk of being kidnapped and sold to plantations in the south. To further protect their identity, Frederick and Anna adopted the surname Johnson and traveled north to New Bedford, Massachusetts, to live and work in a primarily Quaker community known for its strict adherence to racial equality.

Even here, though, where he enjoyed the dignity of a workingman who earned—and kept—an honest wage, the specter of what Frederick called the "Christianity of America" reared its ugly head. In Frederick's view, it had nothing to do with the "Christianity of Christ"—that is, biblical Christianity—but was rather an accommodation made with institutionalized slavery, which in effect nullified the word of God for the sake of human tradition (Mark 7:13). However, Frederick desired to maintain a personal relationship with the Lord. "Among my first concerns on reaching New Bedford was to become united with the church, for I had never given up, in reality, my religious faith."

But his faith would be tested again and again.

After observing a local Methodist minister segregating the few black parishioners from the white ones in his church during the sacrament of Holy Communion, Frederick left that church in search of another. And another. While there may have been a degree of harmony between the races in New Bedford during the workweek, a dividing wall of separation, even hostility, typified church attendance on Sunday mornings.

Frederick finally found a home at the African Methodist Episcopal Zion Church, where he became a licensed preacher in 1839. His religious fervor was rekindled as he held various positions in this church, including Sunday school superintendent and sexton. And his study of the Bible deepened.

After he and Anna had been living in New Bedford for almost half a year, their surname now changed from Johnson to Douglass, Frederick became familiar with antislavery advocate William Lloyd Garrison and his influential newspaper, *The Liberator*. "*The Liberator* was a paper after my own heart," Frederick wrote. "It preached human brotherhood, denounced oppression, and, with all the solemnity of God's word, demanded the complete emancipation of my race."

Frederick began attending abolitionist lectures in New Bedford and surrounding towns and villages. Seeing how extensively Garrison and other abolitionists drew on the Bible to make their case against slavery, he began to cherish anew the word of prophecy spoken years before by his dear Father Lawson—that God had a great work for him to do, and that he would one day preach the gospel to the entire world.

What had Father Lawson said? *God would make a way.* And had not the journey already begun?

The hardworking, thoughtful Frederick attended as many abolitionist meetings as he could. He preferred at first to sit quietly in the rear of the lecture hall but in time was drawn into the fray as an active participant. Word of his preaching abilities spread to the white leaders of the abolitionist movement, several of whom saw the immediate benefit of engaging him as a speaker. Having been born into slavery and having escaped only recently to the north, Frederick was a living "graduate of the peculiar institution" of slavery with his "diploma" written in the scars on his back. Unsure of himself at first, Frederick rose quickly to the task, viewing it as fulfillment of Father Lawson's prophetic word. His natural—and developing—skills as an orator began to elicit strong responses from audiences wherever he spoke. "The God of Israel is with us," he shared in his autobiography. "The might of the Eternal is on our side. Now let the truth be spoken and a nation will start forth at the sound!" Like an Old Testament prophet, Frederick could no longer contain the fire in his belly. He had to speak. He had to act. "In this enthusiastic spirit, I dropped into the ranks of freedom's friends and went forth to the battle."

For the next four years, Frederick served as a public lecturer for the abolitionist movement. He was a riveting speaker who possessed a rich, baritone voice and a commanding physical presence. People most often asked him to simply share the details of his personal story, which he did with alacrity. But he was also eager to expose the fiendishness of slavery from a philosophical, moral, and theological perspective. His arguments were compelling and his manner of speaking so erudite that people began questioning whether he had, in fact, ever been a slave. The innuendo and second-guessing of others led Frederick to write his first autobiography—*Narrative of the Life of Frederick Douglass*—which created an immediate stir. It sold thousands of copies within months and was subsequently translated into French and Dutch.

Frederick's notoriety grew well beyond the borders of Massachusetts, and with it came the fear that his previous owners might attempt to recapture him. It was deemed expedient, therefore, and also helpful to the cause, that he should travel to the British Isles to pull back the curtain on race relations in the United States and engage the support of the British people in eradicating slavery.

From the beginning to the end of his nearly two-year sojourn in Great Britain and Ireland, Frederick made his first and strongest appeal to end slavery on the basis of Christian principle. He declared to rapt listeners crowded in churches and lecture halls throughout Great Britain that

> while America is printing tracts and Bibles and sending missionaries abroad to convert the heathen . . . the slave not only lies forgotten and uncared for, but is trampled underfoot by the very churches of the land . . . Instead of preaching the gospel against this tyranny, ministers of religion have sought by all and every means to throw in the background whatever in the Bible could be construed as opposition to slavery. This I conceive to be the darkest feature of slavery, and the most difficult to attack, because it is identified with religion and exposes those who denounce it to the charge of infidelity.

As Frederick exposed the evils of slavery, through both reason and the gripping details of his personal story, support for emancipation arose in every corner of the United Kingdom—especially from the pulpit. The Reverend Dr. John Campbell, Congregationalist minister of Whitefield's Tabernacle in London, spoke for hundreds of thousands of Britons when he declared in response to one of Frederick's addresses, "My blood boiled within me when I heard his address tonight . . . Let him travel over the island—east, west, north and south—everywhere diffusing knowledge and awakening principle, till the whole nation become a body of petitioners to America. He will, he must, do it. He must for a season make England his home."

And so he did. But there were also those who questioned whether or not he was undermining the cause of Christ by airing the church's dirty laundry in public.

Frederick was adamant in his response.

I love the religion of our blessed Savior. I love that religion that comes from above . . . that is full of mercy and good fruits . . . that sends its votaries to bind up the wounds of him that has fallen among thieves . . . that makes it the duty of its disciples to visit the fatherless and the widow in their affliction. I love that religion that is based upon the glorious principle of love to God and love to man; which makes its followers do unto others as they themselves would be done by. It is because I love this religion that I hate the slaveholding, the woman-whipping, the soul-destroying religion that exists in the southern states of America . . . It is because I regard the one as good, pure and holy that I cannot but regard the other as bad, corrupt and wicked. Loving the one, I must hate the other; holding to the one, I must reject the other.

Frederick gained many supporters while in Great Britain and Ireland. Among them was a Quaker family that volunteered to raise funds to purchase his freedom. Some criticized the undertaking, saying it gave tacit approval to the erroneous premise that one man can, indeed, own another. But Frederick gave the plan a quiet go-ahead. He knew he could accomplish more for the cause if he were free in body as well as spirit.

Intermediaries in New York contacted the Auld family, who agreed to sell. The situation, however, was complicated by the fact that both of the Auld brothers had previously "owned" Frederick. Thomas Auld, therefore, was required to transfer legal ownership of Frederick to Hugh, and Frederick's sale price was set at £150 ($750). A few months later, on December 12, 1846, with the money raised and the purchase complete, Hugh Auld went to the Baltimore County courthouse to formally register a bill of manumission for "Frederick Baily, otherwise called Frederick Douglass." Frederick was now "entirely and legally free" at the age of twenty-eight.

What would he do now? The British Isles and its people had treated him kindly. For the first time ever, as Martin Luther King Jr. might have put it, his skin color was overlooked in deference to the content of his character. He was considered a man in every sense of the word, an equal among equals. "I can truly say I have spent some of the happiest moments of my life since landing in this country," he wrote. "I seem to have undergone a transformation. I live a new life . . . [Here] they measure and esteem men according to their moral and intellectual worth, and not according to the color of their skin."

Frederick had previously thought of bringing his wife and children to England. But with his freedom secure, his next steps seemed clear. "I felt that I had a duty to perform, and that was to labor and suffer with the oppressed in my native land."

Once he was back in the United States, and again helped by friends in Great Britain, Frederick started an abolitionist newspaper called *The North Star*. The paper's motto was, "Right is of no sex, truth is of no color, God is the Father of us all, and we are all brethren."

For the next half-century, Frederick labored tirelessly for human rights. Abolition of slavery, the right of women to vote and hold political office, equal protection under the law, and school desegregation were the main issues that occupied his attention and efforts. He often took a practical, middle-of-the road approach on the issues of the day, steering clear of violence within the abolitionist movement, while at the same time pressing relentlessly for lasting political solutions. At a lecture before a women's rights group in Rochester, New York, he famously said, "I would unite with anybody to do right and with nobody to do wrong." He held numerous public offices during his lifetime and—without his approval—was nominated for vice president of the United States on the Equal Rights Party ticket in 1872.

He also continued to hold firmly to his Christian faith. In 1877, when he was nearly sixty years old and had recently been appointed United States marshal for the District of Columbia, he paid a visit to his old master, Thomas Auld, in St. Michaels, Maryland.

It had been forty years since the two had seen each other. Mr. Auld, who by this time was in his eighties and bedridden, had heard that Frederick was visiting the area. He was also aware that his daughter Amanda had been in touch with him after enthusiastically attending several of his lectures in Philadelphia. The former master invited the former slave to come for a visit. Initially, Frederick had his misgivings but in the end accepted the invitation.

Another one of Auld's daughters, Louisa, and her husband, William Bruff, met Frederick at the door of the family home. They led Frederick to the former master's bedroom and ushered him inside.

> We addressed each other simultaneously [wrote Frederick], he calling me "Marshal Douglass" and I, as I had always called him, "Captain Auld." Hearing myself called by him "Marshal Douglass," I instantly broke up the formal nature of the meeting by saying, "not *Marshal*, but Frederick to you as formerly." We shook hands cordially, and in the act of doing so, he, having been long stricken with palsy, shed tears as men thus afflicted will do when excited by any deep emotion. The sight of him, the changes which time had wrought in him, his tremulous hands constantly in motion, and all the circumstances of his condition affected me deeply, and for a time choked my voice and made me speechless. We both, however, got the better of our feelings, and conversed freely about the past.

Frederick asked his former master what he thought about his conduct in running away and going north. "I always knew you were too smart to be a slave," replied Mr. Auld. "Had I been in your place, I should have done the same."

"I'm glad to hear you say so, Captain Auld," replied Frederick. "After all, I did not run away from you, but from slavery."

"I never did like slavery," confessed Mr. Auld. "It was always my intention to set my slaves free at the age of twenty-five."

The two men continued to converse amicably for nearly half an hour. Here they were, former enemies now reconciled as brothers in Christ. Mr. Auld gripped Frederick's hand and spoke of a better life in heaven.

"Our courses had been determined for us, not by us," wrote Frederick. "We had both been flung, by powers that did not ask our consent, upon a mighty current of life, which we could neither resist nor control. By this current he was a master, and I a slave; but now our lives were verging towards a point where differences disappear, where even the constancy of hate breaks down, where the clouds of pride, passion, and selfishness vanish before the brightness of infinite light."

Frederick ended the visit quietly and left the house. A few weeks later, Captain Auld died peacefully in his sleep. His death gained some attention in the nation's press due to his previous relationship with the now-famous and influential Frederick Douglass.

On February 20, 1895, in Washington, DC, Frederick himself made the journey home to his Maker. There was now laid up for him—the former slave who had first tasted freedom in the sweet embrace of Jesus Christ—a crown of righteousness from his Lord and Judge.

The year is 1981, nine years after my experience in Austin, Texas, that soured me to Christianity. I am at the International Christian Center in Staten Island, New York, a Pentecostal charismatic church where more than a thousand worshipers are in attendance.

I don't want to cry, but I can't help it. As is fitting for a church in New York City, the International Christian Center is a "United Nations" of ethnicities—red, yellow, black, and white—and somehow, we're all precious in his sight.

I think it's the choir that gets to me most. They don't sing in the stoic fashion I associate with childhood. They worship and celebrate! They freely express a love for God that extends to everyone around them. And that love flows down like the oil on Aaron's beard, making itself felt in the sanctuary (see Ps. 133). The preceding nine years have taken their toll on me. I have wandered far from God and now am experiencing rebirth. Here there is forgiveness. There is acceptance in the house of the Lord.

Hands from the nations are laid on my shoulders, prayers are made for my healing, and I cry.

Years ago I had theorized that perhaps God was missing from my life. I also concluded that I would never find him in a Christian church. But I did. I discovered, in the words of Frederick Douglass, that "truth is of no color; that God is the Father of us all."

FLORENCE NIGHTINGALE

It was a strange impulse. My grandmother Weesie, whom I had loved, I think, more than any living soul, had been dead for almost a year. I was about twelve years old at the time. Still grieving her passing, I found a quiet room in my house and knelt down to pray. That in itself was not unusual. As a child I had a sincere belief in God, which I could trace in many ways directly to my grandmother's influence. A precise recollection of what followed fails me, but as I knelt on the floor that day, my heart filled with thoughts of Weesie. I felt a physical sensation that God was with me. That he was hovering over me and had somehow joined himself to me. I even had the feeling that he was directing me to say the words, "God, let me help people."

That was it. A prayer of five words. I don't know if I have ever prayed since with such faith and sincerity. What could have prompted such a prayer?

I believe my grandmother must have had a lot to do with it. To this day, it's hard to think of a gentler, kinder soul. I learned recently from my sister that when Weesie was a young woman growing up in New Mexico, she had planned on becoming a nun. But it wasn't meant to be. She met a man from Chicago who had come to New Mexico to become a painter. They married and had one child—my mother.

I would sometimes spend the weekend at Weesie's small house, which was situated about two miles from my own. (She had moved to Tampa from New Mexico a few years before I was born.) I could share with you many cherished memories of this dear woman. I often saw her praying, and she taught me to pray as well. When I was sick or sad or aggrieved, I could count on her quiet presence to calm and soothe me. She never preached a sermon, but I knew she believed in God. Suffice it to say that I felt her love for me and that her love inspired me to love others.

Who knows what happened that day in Tampa, Florida, when a twelve-year-old boy, mourning the loss of his grandmother, knelt down in a quiet room to pray and spoke five distinct and utterly sincere words to a God he could not see.

He wasn't the first to experience such a phenomenon, as our next story demonstrates.

IMAGINE A HONEYMOON lasting long enough for two children to be born before the newlyweds think of returning home! Or does that even qualify as a "honeymoon"? For the wealthy upper classes of Great Britain in the early nineteenth century, evidently it did. William Edward Nightingale (known by his initials W.E.N.) and his bride, Frances "Fanny" Smith, spent nearly four years in Italy following their high society wedding in 1817. Their first child, Parthenope, was born in 1819 and named after the ancient Greek colony that gave rise to the city of Naples. Their second child, also a girl, was born a year later and likewise named after the city of her birth—Florence.

When Florence (or "Flo," as she was affectionately called) was a year old, her parents decided it was finally time to return home. At first the young family took up residence at W.E.N.'s ancestral home in northern England, a great manor called Lea Hurst, but Fanny deemed the property inadequate with only fifteen bedrooms. Plus, the winters in Derbyshire were harsh. Fanny had decided they needed something more fitting to their station, something in the warmer climes near London, and so the family purchased a second home—a mansion in Hampshire called Embley Park. Here, the Nightingales would spend the fall and winter months, while Lea Hurst would become their summer home.

Flo and Parthe, it is safe to say, lived enchanted lives. Both estates included magnificent woods and gardens to explore, all manner of pets to coddle and farm animals to run after, a large and extended family that paid regular visits, and a seemingly endless parade of distinguished visitors. The girls received excellent educations, at first through a series of governesses, and later by their erudite father, a graduate of Cambridge University. W.E.N. had no "day job," as it were, and poured himself into his daughters' intellectual development, teaching them foreign languages (including classical Greek and Latin), philosophy, history, geography, physics, and mathematics.

Flo was the more natural student of the two. She began writing her autobiography in French at the age of eight. But for the Nightingale children, learning included more than academic pursuits. Each day, in addition to their core studies, the sisters were expected to draw, practice the piano, do needlework or make small gifts by hand, read the Bible, and memorize poetry.

They were also expected to be, as the Bible says, "rich in good deeds." When Flo was a child, country manors in England functioned under a system of patronage in which the local squire (in this case, W.E.N.) looked after the welfare of the families clustered in the surrounding hamlets. Encouraged by their parents, Flo and Parthe helped distribute food and clothing to those who had fallen on hard times. They also performed household chores for the elderly and often nursed the sick. Here again, Flo led the way, finding fulfillment in serving others. "The people about here are very fond of her," wrote Parthe in a letter to her grandmother, "and she likes them and is always sorry to leave them."[1] Her mother, who had long encouraged Flo's philanthropic impulses, was beginning to wonder if she had pushed too hard. The story is told of Fanny taking a lantern one evening to look for her missing daughter and finding her at a poor villager's house, "sitting by the bedside of someone who was ill and saying she could not sit down to a grand seven o'clock dinner."[2]

Now in her teens, Flo had become a physically attractive young woman—tall for her age, slender and graceful, with wavy auburn hair, penetrating hazel-grey eyes, and a beautiful smile. She could also be strong-willed and rebellious. Her parents worried about her because she wasn't like most other girls. She wasn't even much like her own sister and mother. She tended to take after her father, preferring his quiet world of books and learning. But in this respect, too, she was different. By his own choice, W.E.N. had no regular occupation. Why work if you don't need to? Flo, however, longed for a purpose in life. She wanted to make a difference in the world. And why not? She possessed a keen mind, physical courage, and a first-rate education. Through her family connections she had access to the nation's highest echelons of power. But to what end? Girls in nineteenth-century England, even those of the privileged upper classes, had no pathway to a career outside the confines of hearth and home. A woman's place—her only place—was with her family. Women had no right to vote or hold political office. They lost control over their lives and personal property the moment they married. It all created, sometimes quite literally, a maddening situation. Flo knew of several women, friends of her mother, who had suffered mental breakdowns due to the suffocating strictures society placed on them. "I craved for some regular occupation," wrote Flo in one of her autobiographical notes. "For something worth doing, instead of frittering time away on useless trifles."[3] But what would that something be? And how would she recognize it when it came? Flo began to pray.

From the age of six, she began writing down her prayers and keeping track of the answers. In terms of religious observance, both sides of Flo's family outwardly identified with the Church of England and had a strong Unitarian tradition, which surely influenced her social activism and lifetime of good works. But Unitarianism—essentially an antitrinitarian creed—left Flo dissatisfied, for it rejected the divinity of Christ and the personhood of the Holy Spirit. To Flo it was a "dull" doctrine that did nothing to make God "more loved or loveable."[4] She was more attracted to the medieval mystics of the Catholic tradition, who cultivated the spiritual disciplines of fasting, meditation, and prayer, and the down-to-earth teachings of John Wesley, whom she greatly admired. Jesus Christ was at the heart of her spiritual life, and she wrote of being "converted" in 1836 after reading *The Cornerstone*, a book by an American Congregational minister named Jacob Abbott.

Fanny, meanwhile, was making her characteristically emphatic plans for the future. Her daughters would soon be coming out as London debutantes, which, of course, necessitated major upgrades at Embley Park. The only drawback was that the renovations would take months to complete. Why not travel to Europe during the remodeling process? It would do everyone good, Fanny reasoned. The girls could practice their languages and shop for clothes in Paris, while W.E.N. visited old friends in France and Italy and poked about in all the museums. Everyone was enchanted with the idea except Flo.

In January 1837, a flu epidemic spread throughout southern England. In the Nightingale household, only Flo and the chief cook escaped infection, and Flo found herself fully engaged—and never happier—nursing the sick around her. She acquitted herself well, too, as everyone under her care eventually recovered. "I have killed no patients," Flo wrote tongue-in-cheek.[5]

And then, just as the worst of the flu was behind her, Flo had a most unusual experience. She heard a voice calling her in the night. But it was not just any voice. "On February 7, 1837," she wrote in a private note, "God spoke to me and called me to his service."[6] Flo was in the habit of praying and communing daily with God. But this was something else, something distinct. Over the course of her long life, she would chronicle only three other similar incidents. What had happened? Had she heard God's audible voice? And the "call to service"? What did that entail? We can only speculate, since Flo did not elaborate further in her notes. However, over the next six months she spent more time than before serving the poor villagers surrounding Lea Hurst, helping where she could. Fanny no doubt breathed a sigh of relief when September rolled around and Flo obediently joined the family on its European tour.

It was a trip to remember, reminiscent of W.E.N. and Fanny's extended honeymoon years before. The Nightingale family spent eighteen months altogether in Italy, France, and Switzerland, rubbing shoulders with the elite of European society. It was a heady, fairy-tale experience for the girls. Among other adventures, they attended lavish balls and soirees, frequented the opera and theater, and took singing and dance lessons. Fanny was ecstatic at Flo's progress in the social graces.

Flo, however, was less sure of herself. It had been two years since God had "spoken" to her. Why the silence since then? The answer seemed clear enough. She felt she had neglected him amid the siren pleasures of the world—the great balls and operas, *les grandes fêtes*, the flirtations with suitors transporting her to near heavenly realms. A month before the family returned to England, Flo confessed in a private note written from Paris that she could never hope to become a true servant of God until she had overcome "the desire to shine in society."[7] But it seemed an unending struggle, further complicated by the attentions of one highly eligible bachelor named Richard Monckton Milnes. He was ten years her senior, an only son and heir to a great fortune. By all accounts he was a brilliant, genial man with philanthropic interests and a great political future. No one in Flo's family could understand her reluctance to accept his repeated marriage offers. Flo herself could find no good reason, other than the notion that married life would be inimical to her call to God's service. She couldn't bring herself to end the relationship, however, and so it continued.

Finally, at the age of twenty-five, Flo became convinced of her calling or at least had gained enough confidence to make her plans known to W.E.N. and Fanny.

Flo had decided to become a nurse and asked her parents for permission to work at nearby Salisbury Infirmary. Most modern-day parents would welcome such news, but W.E.N. and Fanny were aghast. "It was as if I had wanted to be a kitchen-maid," wrote Flo, describing her parents' reaction.[8]

In truth, it was worse than that. In nineteenth-century England, nursing occupied a rung in society roughly equivalent to that of a streetwalker. There was no concept of a nurse being taught to clinically perform her duties. Only people from the lowest class of society took up such an occupation. Hospitals were known to be places rank with disease and dirt more than places of healing. To cope with the degrading environment, nurses often drank too much and were open to sexual advances by patients and doctors alike. W.E.N. and Fanny thought Flo was mad to consider such a pursuit.

Flo, however, was not one to give up easily. God had spoken to her years before. She was sure of it. How could she disobey the heavenly vision? What did the Gospels say? Had not Christ enjoined his followers to forsake all—even one's family—to follow him? Perhaps she should leave the Church of England and become a nun.

It was in this context that Flo learned of the Institute for Protestant Deaconesses at Kaiserswerth, Germany, near Düsseldorf. Nothing like it existed in England, and it had a spotless reputation for piety and good works. Here Flo would be able to serve honorably alongside other single women dedicated to nursing the sick in a Christian setting.

However, W.E.N. and Fanny still opposed the idea, and Flo, bound by the social conventions of the time, submitted to their authority. That did not keep her from pouring out her anguish in endless notes of self-examination and bitter self-reproach. Her soul had been left in hell, she lamented. Why was God chastising her? Why was he repeatedly putting barriers in her path and preventing her from doing his will? She loved the world too much, she reasoned. She sought the praise of people more than the praise of God. Perhaps she should marry after all. Were not two better than one?

A well-meaning friend suggested to her that she become a writer. But she didn't want to write. "I think one's feelings waste themselves in words," she wrote in an autobiographical note. "They ought all to be distilled into actions and into actions which bring results."[9]

Another family friend encouraged her to accept her secondary role in life as a woman, a helpmate to man, and reminded her that any activity—even a house party—done with the right heart can be to God's glory. Flo was indignant.

"How can it be to the glory of God," she answered, "when there is so much misery in the world which we might be curing, instead of living in luxury?"[10]

Meanwhile, Richard Monckton Milnes wanted an answer. Would Flo marry him? He had waited seven years and refused to wait any longer. What was her decision? With no assurance that she would ever fulfill her calling, with no clear way forward, Flo broke off the relationship. She had thrown herself on the mercies of God and was determined to bring him glory, whether in life or in death. Soon afterward, her health began to decline precipitously, and everyone in her family feared for her sanity.

Fate intervened through family friends Charles and Selina Bracebridge, who invited Flo to accompany them on a trip to Egypt. The Bracebridges understood Flo better than her parents did and arranged for her to train as a nurse at the Institute of St. Vincent de Paul in Alexandria. Flo's spirits revived.

On May 12, 1850, Florence wrote from near Cairo, "Today I am thirty—the age Christ began his mission. Now no more childish things, no more vain things, no more love, no more marriage. Now, Lord, let me only think of Thy will, what Thou willest me to do. Oh Lord, Thy Will, Thy Will."[11]

On the return trip to England, Flo had the chance to visit Kaiserswerth in person. She found it to be all she had hoped for and more, but if she had expected her family to share in her enthusiasm, she was bound for disappointment. Fanny was unrelenting in her desire—rather, her demand—that Flo forsake all such pretensions, while Parthe, her mother's lieutenant and chief enforcer, pressured Flo to embrace the life of ease and privilege into which they had been born and bred. Flo, who always aimed to please her family, bewailed her failures, perceived and unperceived.

"Why, oh my God, cannot I be satisfied with the life that satisfies so many people?" she wrote. "I am told that the conversation of all these good, clever men ought to be enough for me. Why am I starving, desperate, diseased on it? What is the cause of it? My God what am I to do?"[12]

Finally, Flo received an answer when W.E.N., perhaps against his better judgment, became her secret ally. Who knows what his thought process may have been? He was very much a man of his time, yet seems to have become increasingly resigned to the unorthodox course of his daughter's genius, a genius he had recognized and nourished from her earliest years. He could not refuse her pleas to return to Kaiserswerth for meaningful service to others.

Flo went back to the institute in 1851 for three months of nurse's training. She divided her time between working with children in the orphan asylum and assisting everywhere she could in the hospital, including with surgeries. Prayer, Bible study, and hearty Christian fellowship undergirded every aspect of service at Kaiserswerth. Flo had arrived. "Now I know what it is to live and to love life," she wrote of her experience.[13]

Fanny and Parthe remained unconvinced. After Flo returned to England, they remonstrated with her to return to life as she knew it at Embley Park and Lea Hurst. Their appeals fell on deaf ears. As was true with Mary, who stayed at Jesus' feet, Flo had chosen that better part, and it would not be taken from her (Luke 10:42). She went on to gain additional work experience at a Catholic-run hospital outside Paris. And in 1853, she assumed the role of unpaid superintendent at a London hospital for governesses with the quaint name, the Institution for the Care of Sick Gentlewomen in Distressed Circumstances.

In characteristic fashion, she threw all her energy into her new position and performed her duties exceptionally well. The enthusiastic approval of some of the family's most influential society friends further enhanced her reputation, which tamped down on Fanny's objections. Justifiably proud of his daughter, W.E.N. bequeathed her an annual income of £500, which allowed her to live comfortably and pursue her work unhindered. Perhaps Flo's story would have ended here, as a footnote on women pioneers in the medical field, had fate not taken another twist.

Enter the Crimean War (1853–1856), which some have described as one of the most bungled military campaigns the British Empire ever waged. That may be too harsh a characterization, the disastrous Charge of the Light Brigade notwithstanding. It was, in fact, the first ever "media war," in which newspaper correspondents—utilizing the newfangled telegraph machine and black-and-white photography—crafted with frenetic intensity the narrative that made its way home to the British public. It was not a pretty picture, but what war ever is?

Sick and wounded soldiers typically had to wait for days or weeks to make the voyage from Crimea across the Black Sea to Constantinople (modern Istanbul), where they were loaded onto carts or mules for the grueling trip to the Scutari Barracks—a temporary military hospital woefully lacking in medical supplies and basic hygiene. Scutari had no running water, no chairs or tables, not even an operating table. When the straw-stuffed beds ran out, the wounded were placed on the vermin-infested floor and never washed or attended to. Essentially, they were left to die. The Reverend Sidney Godolphin Osborne recounted kneeling by these men to write down their dying messages and finding his notepaper covered with lice.

The reporting of William Howard Russell from the *Times* of London was typical of the newspaper accounts creating a furor back in England: "Not only are men kept, in some cases, for a week without the hand of a medical man coming near the wounds," wrote Russell, "not only are they left to expire in agony, unheeded and shaken off . . . but now, when they are placed in the spacious building where we were led to believe that everything was ready which could ease their pain or facilitate their recovery, it is found that the commonest of appliances of a workhouse sick-ward are wanting."[14]

The British public was further incensed that wounded French soldiers were receiving far better care at their military hospitals, which were attended by Catholic Sisters of Charity. "Why didn't England have something similar?" an aggrieved nation cried. "Where are our English Sisters of Charity?"

In the course of the national debate, Flo was galvanized into action and wrote a letter to her close friend, Liz Herbert, wife of Sidney Herbert, Britain's war secretary, volunteering her services. Coincidentally, Secretary Herbert had already written Flo to ask for her help in coordinating a nursing relief effort. Their letters had crossed in the mail.

After going back and forth on the number of nurses needed, the two settled on forty. Thirty-eight eventually made the two-week trip by sea. Flo handpicked each person and included eight Anglican and ten Catholic sisters.

Flo's official title was Superintendent of the Female Nursing Establishment of the English General Hospitals in Turkey.

It could have included a hundred more fancy words and appellations but wouldn't have made a whit of difference to the skeptical, all-male military medical establishment already in place and struggling to keep its head above water. Flo was a trespasser—an incursion—in a man's world. She and her nurses were simply not welcome. Upon arrival at Scutari they were consigned a barren kitchen and five rat-infested bedrooms in which to live. Adding insult to injury, they were ordered to refrain from contact with the sick and dying soldiers.

Five days later, however, the wounded began pouring in from the Battles of Balaklava and Inkerman. The barracks hospital was completely overwhelmed, and Flo and her nurses were called into action.

She promptly mandated new standards of care, requiring that every wounded soldier be bathed, his wounds bandaged with clean dressing, and his bed linens washed and changed regularly. The need for proper ventilation and sanitation on the wards was addressed and latrine pipes unclogged. Staff members organized the limited medical supplies, and Flo made sure the soldiers received hot and healthy meals, even as she lobbied through her contacts back in Britain for funds to purchase more fresh food and medical supplies. Through it all, she herself set the pattern for her nurses to follow, sometimes on her feet for twenty-four hours at a stretch, or on her knees dressing wounds for up to eight hours at a time. She had no secretary to help with administrative work, yet she managed to keep scrupulously detailed accounts of hospital-related business. She and her "sisters" also helped the soldiers write letters home.

When the nurses retired for the night, Flo would continue making her rounds, typically carrying a lamp in front of her.

She would go from bed to bed checking on each man, voicing a comforting word, whispering a prayer. The soldiers adored her; they knew she was their champion and would fight for them to receive the best care humanly possible. They began calling her "the lady with the lamp," a fitting sobriquet picked up by the ever-present war correspondents, who all agreed that Florence Nightingale was the only true hero to emerge from the Crimean War.

Five months after the war ended with the Treaty of Paris in 1856, Flo quietly returned to England. She was now at peace with her family. Even the Queen paid her visits. But instead of resting on her laurels, Flo set to work adapting the research and field experience she had gathered during her time in Turkey to address much-needed reform in England's military hospitals. In 1858, she became the first woman elected as a fellow of the Royal Statistical Society. In 1860, she established the Nightingale Training School for Nurses, which is still in operation today.

During her lifetime, Flo published two hundred books, reports, and pamphlets. In 1883, Queen Victoria awarded her the Royal Red Cross, and in 1907, the queen's successor, King Edward VII, bestowed on her the Order of Merit for her extraordinary achievements in the field of medicine. Flo was the first woman ever to receive the award.

Though she was often ill for much of the remainder of her life (a side effect of her service at Scutari), Florence lived to be ninety years old. She never married.

She nursed both her parents during their final days, and finally her sister, Parthe, who died in 1890. There were no children to sit by Flo's bedside when her own time on earth was drawing to a close in August 1910. As the end came, though, she was able to say with characteristic resolve and good cheer, "I have fought the good fight, I have finished the race, and I have remained faithful. And now the prize awaits me—the crown of righteousness, which the Lord, the righteous Judge, will give me on the day of his return. And the prize is not just for me but for all who eagerly look forward to his appearing" (2 Tim. 4:7–9 NLT).

I can relate on a personal level to Flo "hearing" from God and waiting many years for the calling to become clear.

In my case, fifteen years had passed since that day following my grandmother's death when I prayed, "God, let me help people." I was married without children and living in New York City, thinking often about how I could make it in the world. I had graduated from film school at New York University and was trying every angle I could think of to break into the movie business. I was also exploring the world of spirituality, studying metaphysics, delving into the occult, and reading the holy books of various religions. I called it my "search for truth."

I had been practicing meditation for a year or so and was sitting cross-legged on my apartment floor reading an issue of the *Village Voice* when one article in particular caught my attention. It was a report about an outdoor meeting in Greenwich Park in which an Indian guru named Swami Muktananda had held a rally a few weeks prior. During the rally he had shared his spiritual insights with a crowd that had gathered around him and had "blessed" the people with the touch of his peacock feather. Witnesses reported several people falling to the ground, overcome by a sense of all-encompassing love and joy. Others claimed they were physically and emotionally healed.

Suddenly, without warning, I burst into tears. Amid loud cries and sobbing, I shouted out, "God, why am I not helping people?"

Let me be clear. This is not an endorsement of Swami Muktananda, who died a few years later in 1982. It is simply a statement of fact. One day I was reading a newspaper account about a "holy" man doing good to people when the memory of my childhood prayer came forcefully to mind. The years had passed, and I felt as though I had done nothing to help anyone. Why? From where I stood—or sat, in this instance—I felt as though God had not answered my prayer. And for the life of me, I couldn't figure out why.

Fast forward to October 1981. I have finished reading the Bible from cover to cover and am drawn to the life of Christ. I want to be a Christian but still have some doubts and questions. Again, I remember my childhood prayer. But this time, I get an answer: "You want to help people. But there's something you need to do first. You need to let me help you."

Crying in relief and joy—my, how I can cry!—I bow my head by the gently flowing river and give my life to Christ. An hour or so later I get to my feet and walk away. I figure my life as a filmmaker is over. What will I do for a living? It doesn't matter. I am for God, and God is for me.

Let the journey begin.

FRANK PAÍS

In 1961, a middle-aged woman named María Escobar
came to live with my family. She was from the village of
San Luis near Cuba's second-largest city, Santiago de
Cuba. Her father had owned a farm there, and María and
members of her family, including at least one brother
and three sisters, had immigrated to the United States
following Fidel Castro's rise to power.

María was a single woman and didn't speak a word of
English. As I walked into the kitchen that first morning,
dressed and ready for school, my mother introduced us
and told me that María would be living in our home. (My
mother was of Hispanic origin, born and raised in New
Mexico, and fluent in Spanish.)

I didn't understand the full extent of the situation
at first. I had a vague understanding of the problems
that existed between the United States and Cuba at the
time and knew that María (and many other Cubans) had
come to the United States seeking refuge from turmoil

at home. I also understood that she'd be helping my mother with child care and household duties. The bottom line was that she was now a member of our family and would, in fact, live with us for the next thirty years before moving to her own house a few miles down the road.

As a child, I didn't always get along with María. It seemed to me she acted too much like a policewoman when my mother wasn't around. My Spanish improved dramatically, though, as I learned to "defend" myself in my juvenile negotiations with her.

But those rough patches were only a small part of the story. I spent many more hours talking pleasantly with María about the Cuba she knew and loved. Growing up close to Santiago de Cuba as she did, I have to wonder if she knew the man featured in our next biography— Frank País. Most people living in Cuba in the 1950s— especially near Santiago de Cuba—knew about the young *santiagüero* who had fearlessly stood up to the Cuban dictator, Fulgencio Batista. He faced the Goliath of his time and was, in many ways, like King David of the Bible—a man after God's own heart.

DRESSED IN GREEN MILITARY FATIGUES with semiautomatic rifles slung over their shoulders, the *guerrilleros* descended the Sierra Maestra of eastern Cuba as gods. Outnumbered, outgunned for years, they were now improbable victors in a fierce civil war waged against the despised Fulgencio Batista.

In the early morning hours of New Year's Day 1959, Batista packed two airplanes with cash, gold, and treasures of art and flew out of Havana, the country's capital, for Santo Domingo. There fellow dictator Rafael Trujillo had rolled out the red carpet to receive him and his corrupt retinue.

Honor among thieves, after all.

With Batista out of the picture, thirty-two-year-old Fidel Castro Ruz took to center stage. To cement his victory over the Batistiano forces and to encourage national unity, Castro led his *soldados barbudos* ("bearded soldiers") in a victory procession from Santiago de Cuba on the eastern edge of the island west toward Havana—a distance of 540 miles. There was hardly a Cuban on the island who did not turn out to cheer on the victors.

Steely-gazed Huber Matos remained faithfully by Fidel's side during the weeklong journey. They were joined along the way by an eclectic group of Fidel's inner circle, including the Argentine doctor Ernesto "Che" Guevara, with his movie-star good looks and trademark black beret, and the jovial, cigar-smoking Camilo Cienfuegos, who preferred a Stetson cowboy hat for headgear, wearing it at a rakish angle over his black shoulder-length hair. Fidel's younger brother, Raúl, stood patiently at the center of things, somehow less noticeable than the others, but never missing a beat.

Then there were the female freedom fighters—heroines like Haydée Santamaría, Celia Sánchez, and the beautiful and alluring Vilma Espín. These and other women had organized protests in the cities and fought in the Sierra Maestra as equals alongside the men, often proving themselves the better soldiers in the bargain.

Inevitably, some were missing from the lineup of champions—including one who might have been the *comandante* instead of Fidel had time and chance been more kind.

His name was Frank País, a true hero of the Cuban Revolution and an evangelical Christian.

Frank was born in Santiago de Cuba on December 7, 1934. His father, Reverend Francisco País Pesqueira, had been a widower previously, and was seventy-two at the time of Frank's birth. He had immigrated to Cuba in 1907 from Galicia in the northwest corner of Spain and was one of the founding members of the First Baptist Church in Santiago de Cuba. He and his second wife, Rosario García Calviño (also from Galicia), had two more children after Frank—Agustín and Josué.

The País brothers were raised in a loving and stable Christian home, and people across the island highly regarded Reverend País for not only his preaching but also the care he demonstrated for countless widows and orphans, as well as the poor and disenfranchised in the community. Reverend País's compassion for others would be among the greatest aspects of his legacy to his children. When he died in October 1939 at the age of seventy-seven, Frank was not yet five years old.

To be sure, Doña Rosario, who was forty years old when her husband died, had her hands full raising three active boys. Every day she gathered her brood by her side for a time of prayer and Bible reading, and on Sundays she took the boys to church, where she led the choir and played the organ.

Frank became the little "man of the house"—protective of his brothers and deeply devoted to his mother. He was an excellent student and avid reader whose favorite book was the Bible. He had two heroes in life—José Martí and Jesus Christ. The latter needs no introduction. However, a word or two about José Martí might be in order.

First and foremost, it is important to note that Cubans, regardless of political leaning, revere the memory of José Martí, who died in 1895 during Cuba's second war of independence from Spain. Still known today as the "Apostle," Martí is to Cubans what George Washington is to Americans—the father of the country. Like Frank, Martí's parents were Spanish immigrants, and it was not lost on young Frank that his hero's resistance to Spanish rule in Cuba began when he was a teenager. Frank read all of Martí's works and dared to dream that he, too, might one day make a difference in the life of his country.

Frank enjoyed a Christian education. His elementary schooling took place at the appropriately named José Martí Institute, which was a part of his father's church. His mother taught him to play the piano, and he taught himself the accordion, composing hymns and mastering a substantial repertoire of music ranging from classical to folk. He was also a painter, a poet, and a stamp collector.

As he grew older, Frank led Bible studies at church and often preached on Sundays. He was warm and caring by nature. In his spare time, he taught sugarcane workers how to read and write, and like his father, he organized visits to the local jails and hospitals to comfort the suffering.

He was in every respect a model son, and people naturally assumed that he would one day become a pastor like his father. And he probably would have, had tyranny not reared its menacing head.

Since 1940, Cuba had enjoyed a progressive, democratic constitution that ushered in land reform and guaranteed free elections. But as the nation prepared to elect a new president in 1952, military strongman Fulgencio Batista, former president of Cuba (1940–1944), forcibly intervened. It is one of the cruel ironies of history that General Batista, who had worked with all sides to implement his country's original constitution, now chose to cynically dismantle it.

On March 10, 1952, Batista seized control of the military and police, as well as radio and television stations throughout the island. Sitting Cuban president, Carlos Prío Socarrás, fled into exile, and Cuba fell under the absolute control of the former sergeant stenographer who had risen through the ranks to become *El Hombre*—"The Man."

People in Santiago de Cuba were outraged.

Frank, just seventeen years old at the time, led his fellow students at the Oriente Teacher's School in a street protest that called for Batista's arrest and trial. It was one of several spontaneous reactions throughout Cuba to Batista's brazen *coup d'état*. A graduate of the University of Havana Law School, Fidel Castro, did the same.

But the protests would have little impact. Batista consolidated his power, buying the military's allegiance for cash and cozying up with the island's rich and powerful. He cast his government in the light of a "disciplined democracy," banning trade unions and cutting diplomatic ties with the Soviet Union, which pleased the United States. He also censored the press. In the years that followed, he made strategic (and immensely profitable) ties with American mafia figures, while the gap between Cuba's rich and poor continued to widen. Havana became known as the "Latin Las Vegas," a place where prostitution, gambling, and drug trafficking thrived while government officials of every stripe went on the take. To quell growing discontent, *El Hombre* imposed censorship of the press while his secret police waged a reign of terror that eventually claimed the lives of an estimated twenty thousand people. To top it all off, he received financial and military support from the United States, which fell for the argument that Batista stood as a necessary bulwark against the spread of communism in a volatile part of the world.

But Batista's autocratic rule would not go unchallenged. On July 26, 1953, Fidel Castro and a band of supporters attacked the Moncada Barracks on the outskirts of Santiago de Cuba. The attack was meant to ignite a general uprising throughout the island but ended in failure. Castro narrowly avoided execution at the hands of Batista's soldiers and was later imprisoned on the Isle of Pines. While in prison, he formed a revolutionary group called M-26-7, which took its name from the attack on the Moncada Barracks. The "M" stood for *movimiento*, or "movement," followed by the day and month of the attack (26 July).

Batista was now sitting pretty and called for elections in 1954 to have himself voted in, unopposed, as Cuba's president. In a magnanimous gesture toward his foes, he declared a general amnesty on May 8, 1955—a Mother's Day gift, he said, for Cuba's political prisoners. Castro, among others, was free to walk. He lingered in Cuba for a few months but realized his prospects were dim (and his life in danger) and fled to Mexico.

After hearing of Fidel's departure, Batista no doubt lit up a cigar and congratulated himself on having eliminated the last vestige of dissent on the island. He never imagined that a soft-spoken Christian schoolteacher in Santiago de Cuba would prove to be a greater threat to his rule than the fiery and loquacious Fidel.

Following graduation from Oriente Teacher's College the same year as the Moncada uprising, Frank was offered a teaching position at El Salvador Christian School, located on the campus of Santiago de Cuba's Second Baptist Church. Agustín González, the school's headmaster and the church's senior pastor, was eager to have Frank on staff. Frank had earned high marks at school, and the País family was delighted by his newfound opportunity to teach third and fourth grade at El Salvador.

Frank did not disappoint. He worked diligently and introduced several novel approaches to teaching, including sitting among the students during his classroom lectures and allowing them to form their own committees. He gained their trust, much like a pastor might, and helped out when the older boys presented disciplinary problems. Instead of punishing the boys harshly, he took them to the chapel and helped them calm down by playing the piano and praying with them. According to one student, "All the girls were in love with him, all the boys wanted to be like him."[1]

Frank taught at El Salvador for two years. During this time he remained faithful in his activities at church, but he also felt a growing call toward another destiny—that of a revolutionary.

One might instinctively assume Frank had become secular, godless. Not so. He didn't oppose Batista because he had turned from his Christian faith but because he believed it was what his faith demanded of him. The facts were before him. His beloved *patria* had been a pawn of Spanish colonialism for centuries, followed by decades of exploitation by American business interests and organized crime. Homegrown dictators like Batista had repeatedly violated the "inalienable rights" of the Cuban people.

But can a Christian take up arms and remain a true follower of Christ? Is there ever justification for resisting force with force? Ask those founding fathers of the United States who went to war with England. Ask Dietrich Bonhoeffer of Germany, the pastor and theologian who resisted Hitler and aided plans for his assassination. Ask Frank País of the First Baptist Church of Santiago de Cuba. He saw his fellow Cubans suffering cruel oppression, many facing torture and murder at the hands of Batista's secret police, and decided to do something about it.

Like David gathering stones from a stream to fight Goliath, Frank started with what he had available—personal charisma, boundless energy, and loyal friends. He was mature beyond his years and knew how to organize people as a result of his church activities and teaching experience. He formed the *Acción Nacional Revolucionaria* (National Revolutionary Action Party or ANR). It consisted initially of underground cells of students and young working-class folk in Santiago de Cuba. Under Frank's leadership, these youthful revolutionaries-in-training (their average age was seventeen) began storing weapons and medical supplies for a future uprising. They also organized mass street protests and published a small bulletin countering Batista's censored version of the news.

In June of 1955, Frank tendered his resignation at El Salvador. Pastor González asked him to reconsider, but Frank declined, believing—as Martí had—that no personal sacrifice was too great for the good of his country. The reverend could not dissuade him.

Frank hid few of his increasingly radical activities from the purview of his mother. She saw him on a slippery slope, indeed. And worse, he was dragging his younger brothers into the fray. That same summer of 1955, Frank killed a man in an attack on the police station at El Caney. Doña Rosario confronted him, even though—so he claimed—he had acted in self-defense. It didn't matter to his mother. She understood the need for change in Cuba but couldn't condone violence and murder. The Scripture was clear: "All those who take up the sword shall perish by the sword" (Matt. 26:52 NASB). For his part, Frank held to the view that tyranny should be resisted on the basis of personal conscience; that a godly man should "defend the weak and the fatherless; uphold the cause of the poor and the oppressed" (Ps. 82:3 NIV).

The argument subsided when Frank assured his mother he would not resort to violence again. But he had chosen his way, and it would inevitably lead to more bloodshed, as occurred the following year in April, when Frank and his group clashed with the military and police in Santiago de Cuba.

Meanwhile, in Mexico, Castro was making plans to invade Cuba. He gathered close to a hundred supporters around him while Frank took the lead in organizing an uprising in Santiago meant to coincide with Castro's group landing on Cuban soil. Frank traveled twice to Mexico to meet with Fidel in person and lay the groundwork for the invasion. November 30, 1956, was the projected target date.

But as even the casual student of history knows, the most carefully prepared plans can sometimes go awry. Frank's uprising went off as planned on November 30, but Castro's group did not reach the shores of Cuba until two days later and were very nearly wiped out by Batista's waiting soldiers. Only a handful of the rebels—including Fidel, Che Guevara, and Raúl Castro—managed to escape into the mountains. Batista now readied his long knives to end the rebel resistance once and for all.

Los Tigres de Masferrer (the Masferrer Tigers) was a paramilitary death squad organized by Rolando Masferrer, a staunch supporter of Batista. Following the November 30 uprising, Batista gave these trained killers the green light to operate with impunity on the island. The group tortured many innocent people for information and publicly executed hundreds, including young teens. "Mangled bodies were left hanging from lamp posts or dumped in the streets in a grotesque variation of the Spanish colonial practice of public executions."[2]

The cruelty of Batista's henchmen did not go unanswered. There were reprisals during this time—a life for a life—and Frank took on a hero's status in the eyes of ordinary people. A huge bounty was placed on his head. At the same time, young Frank was experiencing an inner conflict that transcended his earthly struggle. That struggle came to light years later when a remarkable poem he wrote toward the end of 1956 was found. In the poem, which could almost be mistaken for a psalm of David, Frank admitted that he'd sinned against heaven and against God. He begged for God's forgiveness and acknowledged God's great mercy, asking for one more chance.[3]

Frank's enemies, of course, had no intention of giving him, or anyone associated with him in the underground, a second chance. In June 1957, police arrested, tortured, and killed Frank's youngest brother, seventeen-year-old Josué. His body was dumped on the streets of Santiago de Cuba.

A month later, Frank suffered the same fate. He was betrayed at what he thought was a safe house, taken into police custody, and executed a few hours later. His killers placed a cocked revolver near his inert hand to give the impression he had died in a shootout with the police. It was a farce and everyone knew it. He had been shot at close range in the back of the head.

The city of Santiago de Cuba came to a standstill. On the day of Frank's funeral, businesses closed and every working citizen went on strike. More than 100,000 people lined the streets of Santiago de Cuba to mourn their fallen hero. General Batista surely must have taken pause. Resistance to his rule had now crossed all ages, classes, and racial lines in Cuba. He had become a despised figure, ruling by unjust means. Even as Frank was being laid to rest near José Martí's earthly remains in the Santa Ifigenia cemetery, Castro's guerrilla forces were engaged in a life-and-death struggle with army regulars in the mountains of the Sierra Maestra. Batista's forces held the advantage . . . for the time being. It was still "the hour when darkness reigned," but Batista's days were numbered.

"Don't worry about the wicked or envy those who do wrong," wrote King David. "For like grass, they soon fade away. Like spring flowers, they soon wither . . . Soon the wicked will disappear. Though you look for them, they will be gone" (Ps. 37:1–2, 10 NLT).

Agustín was now Doña Rosario's sole remaining child. With the aid of the Spanish embassy in Cuba, he was whisked away to Costa Rica, and from there to the United States. Doña Rosario remained in Cuba until her death in 1977.

It is worth speculating what might have happened had Frank lived to see Batista's defeat and the Revolution's victory in 1959. Would he, instead of Castro, have become Cuba's leader? If he had, it's hard to imagine he would have led Cuba down the path to communism. It is much more likely he would have worked as tirelessly to reinstate the Cuban Constitution of 1940 as he had labored to unseat Batista. With Cuba's freedom assured, might Frank then have embarked on his lifelong dream of being an architect? Would he have returned to teaching, or might he have become a pastor like his father? Or perhaps he would have assumed a role in government, which would have been a blessing for the Cuban people. As the proverb says, "When the righteous are in authority, the people rejoice; But when a wicked man rules, the people groan" (Prov. 29:2 NKJV).

Perhaps the prophet Isaiah expressed Frank's fate best when he wrote, "The righteous perish, and no one takes it to heart; the devout are taken away, and no one understands that the righteous are taken away to be spared from evil" (Isa. 57:1).

To put it in more contemporary vernacular, "Only the good die young."

I had the opportunity to travel to Cuba three times in the 1990s. On my third and final trip, I traveled from Havana all the way to Santiago de Cuba and back by car. Not just any car. My traveling companion (a cameraman) and I rented a Mercedes Benz and rode in luxury all the way. We cruised the nearly empty Cuban roads like rock stars, pulling into towns at night where the most fancy vehicles to be seen were American-made Fords and Chevys from the 1950s or box-like Russian Ladas. I had only a dim idea at the time how privileged I was to be making such a trip—certainly as an American.

When it was time to catch my return flight to Mexico City, however, the military police detained me at the José Martí International Airport. Two men—one tall, the other short—questioned me. I'll call them Good Cop and Bad Cop. They knew everything about me—where I was born and raised, where I worked in the States, everyone with whom I had visited during my time in Cuba.

Bad Cop did most of the talking and accused me of having broken numerous Cuban laws by making an unauthorized trip across the island. I protested, saying that I had cleared my travels with the Ministry of Culture. It didn't matter; according to him, and for reasons I couldn't quite follow, I had broken the law. I prayed.

The two rifled through my luggage, which had never reached the plane. Bad Cop picked up my Spanish Bible.

"We're atheists in Cuba," he said, scowling at me. Then he came across a book I had purchased a week earlier—*Fidel and Religion*. "Now this is a good book," he said.

"Yes," I agreed. "A very interesting book. I've been reading it during my trip and praying for Fidel."

Bad Cop grimaced, but I detected a hint of openness on the part of Good Cop. I turned toward him. "God has given me a great love for the Cuban people," I said.

"Why is that?" asked Good Cop.

"Well, I became a Christian twelve years ago, and what I most care about now is sharing God's love with other people."

Bad Cop now found what he had been looking for—several cassette tapes from the videotaping I had done on the island. He held the tapes up in the air. "You have violated Cuban law," he said. "You can go to prison for this!"

It's hard to explain what happened next, but I felt a tangible joy begin to fill my heart. I looked at Good Cop and Bad Cop and saw two men who needed God. Then I shared my testimony with them and asked Good Cop to read several passages aloud from my Bible. I ended up showing them pictures of my family and shaking their hands. Bad Cop sent me to my plane, which had been held on the tarmac for several hours while I was being interrogated. "God loves you" were my last words to them. I never got my tapes back.

Once I was on the airplane, I saw the cameraman who had traveled with me. He glanced at me nervously. For some reason they had not detained him. I settled in my seat, and the plane prepared for takeoff. My body began to tremble.

A year or so later I was in Tampa visiting my parents and paid my usual visit to María Escobar. She was mostly bedridden by then, attended by two of her sisters, who lived with her. I sat by her bed for a while, holding her hand and telling her the story of my detention at the airport in Havana. She squeezed my hand tighter and looked at me with a peaceful expression. I remembered those times I had been sick and she had sat by my side, serving me hot soup and sharing stories of the Cuba of her childhood.

Her tales always ended with a *dicho*, or saying. I remember one phrase particularly well: *Haz bien no mires a quién.* It doesn't have quite the same ring in English but translated means, "Do good without regard to whom."

Now our positions were reversed. It was my turn to tell a story, and as I had done with Good Cop and Bad Cop, I told María about God's great love for us as revealed in Christ. I told her how he had made himself personal to me and how my life had changed because of it. I could tell from the look in her eyes that she understood and was glad to hear what I had to say. Then I held her hand a little tighter and said a prayer.

María died in 2003 at the age of ninety-seven.

She was my first introduction to that beautiful island of violet hues some three hundred miles to the south of Tampa. She birthed in my heart a love for the Cuban people and a desire for their freedom, prosperity, and peace. It's a love affair that continues today with all my heart and soul.

Fyodor Dostoyevsky

I was first introduced to the Russian writer Fyodor Dostoyevsky through his novella *Notes from the Underground*. At the time, I was a sixteen-year-old student at the Lawrenceville School in New Jersey. Dostoyevsky, I was told, was an existentialist writer, and many considered his book to be the first existentialist novel written. A logical next question for me was, What is existentialism?

I never discovered a concise definition, but I did learn that existentialism implies living as best you can in a world without meaning or purpose. For the remainder of my teen years and into my early twenties, I embraced this philosophy as my personal worldview. Dostoyevsky is said to have been a hero to Friedrich Nietzsche, the German philosopher famous for the quote, "God is dead." He was also admired by the atheist Jean-Paul Sartre, as well as other atheist and agnostic writers, for his unflinching view on the depravity of humankind.

It never occurred to me that he might have had faith in a higher power.

THEY WERE SERFS, human chattel, rounded up from the length and breadth of the Russian Empire and marched unceremoniously to the Neva River marshlands by the Baltic Sea. There in 1703, Peter the Great, tsar of Russia, decreed that a new city would be built—one to rival the splendid capitals of Europe and provide Russia its "window to the West." With the help of German engineers, an intricate grid of canals was devised, while every ship that came into port was required to offload tons of earth to help reclaim the swamp. The new metropolis was to be called St. Petersburg. It was named after the tsar's patron saint and incorporated his Western outlook (*burg* is the German word for "city").

The conscripted serf laborers (among them soldiers taken prisoner during Russia's long Northern War with Sweden) performed the backbreaking labor of building the city, dying by the tens of thousands from rampant disease, starvation, bitter cold, and even marauding wolves. Their ultimate sacrifice earned St. Petersburg two sobriquets: "Venice of the North" and a second, less flattering one—the "City of Bones."

The first building constructed on the drained swampland was the massive Peter and Paul Fortress, which housed a small maximum-security prison. One of its first detainees was none other than Tsar Peter's eldest son and heir apparent, Alexei Petrovich, who had been arrested, tortured, and killed for his perceived disloyalty to his father.

Over the ensuing decades, the garrisoned fortress housed a regular succession of political prisoners, among them the

Decembrists (high-ranking military officers who in December 1825 refused allegiance to Tsar Nicholas I) and twenty-five years later the Petrashevsky Circle (a group of utopian Socialists who clamored for an egalitarian Russia and the abolition of serfdom).

Among the imprisoned "agitators" of the Petrashevsky Circle (known collectively as the Petrashevsty) was a young writer who had come to the attention of the Russian literary world in 1846 with his critically acclaimed first novel *Poor Folk*. His second book, *The Double*, did not do as well. While he begged to differ somewhat with the Petrashevsty's embrace of atheism as a core value of their movement, he advocated strongly for liberation of the serfs. However, he had committed the "crime" of spreading antigovernment propaganda by means of a home lithograph machine and now occupied cell number nine in a notorious part of the prison known as the Alekseevsky Ravelin—a triangular fortification built just inside the fortress walls.

The young man's name was Fyodor Dostoyevsky. He was twenty-seven years old at the time of his arrest. Agents of the secret police had been observing him and his coconspirators for several months when they were rounded up in a predawn raid on April 23, 1849. Initially, Fyodor had wondered how long he'd last in solitary confinement. He was high-strung by nature, easily excitable, and in prison suffered from bouts of illness and insomnia.

His quarters were damp and cold. At night an oil lamp sputtered irregularly on a small table near his cot, and during the day faint light entered through a barred window high up the wall, its smeared glass allowing no clear view of the world outside. The young writer fought his growing despair by mentally outlining future novels, and when three months had passed, he and the other prisoners were allowed to have books and writing materials. It was during this time that Fyodor penned a charming short story titled "A Little Hero."

Languishing in his cell, he allowed his mind to wander back to a mostly happy childhood. His mother and father, now deceased, had been deeply devoted to each another and had spread that love to their children. It was a close-knit family marked by a love of learning and devotion to the Orthodox Church. Marya Feodorovna, Fyodor's mother, was known for her no-nonsense approach to life and her deep compassion for the poor and hurting. Early on she taught her children to read from a book of Bible stories.

Fyodor's father, Mikhail Andreevich, was a military surgeon and a stern man, but no less loving in his way. Though short of temper, he never struck his children and was forever preoccupied with their welfare. He tutored them personally and sacrificed financially to send them to the finest schools in Moscow and, later, St. Petersburg.

Perhaps the most pleasant memories of all were wrapped around Darovoe, the family's summer estate, or *dacha*, which Mikhail Andreevich acquired when Fyodor was eight years old. Located ninety miles south of Moscow, Darovoe barely produced a livelihood for the serfs who lived on the property, but it was a place of wonder and excitement to the impressionable Fyodor. Here he left behind the claustrophobic city life and was free to roam the wooded glens and soak up the ways and manners of the poor folk who tilled the land. But Darovoe was far away now. Impossibly far away.

During the first six months of his imprisonment, Fyodor and his fellow Petrashevsty were brought in one by one for questioning before a joint civilian-military Commission of Inquiry. It was clear that no one in the group had done much more than talk about the imperative for social change in Mother Russia and for the need of the people "to be awakened to their own human dignity."[1] But in the turbulent political climate of the late 1840s, with monarchies toppling right and left in Western Europe, mere talk of social change raised deep suspicions, and the reactionary tsar, Nicholas I, was taking no chances. His rule had been threatened at its inception by the Decembrist revolt, and he was determined now to make a statement with his treatment of these erstwhile revolutionaries.

The commission concluded its interrogation in October, and in mid-November, fifteen of the Petrashevsty, including Fyodor, were sentenced to execution by firing squad. That judgment was forwarded for final review to the General-Auditoriat, the nation's highest military court, where an additional eight prisoners were added to the list of the condemned.

And then, almost in the manner of actors in a play, the judges on the General-Auditoriat appealed to the tsar for mercy. It was well known that Nicholas I enjoyed the role of benevolent ruler, especially when it suited his political ends. But what would his final decision be? The prisoners were left in the dark.

Then early on the morning of December 22, Fyodor and his fellow prisoners were ordered to change out of their prison garb and into the civilian clothes they had been wearing when they were first arrested. They were marched outside into the winter chill, and each prisoner was ordered inside a two-seater carriage with an armed escort. Thirty minutes later, surrounded by mounted police, the caravan of carriages arrived in Semyonovsky Square.

Snow had fallen earlier that morning and the ground was a pristine white. In the middle of the square stood a newly erected platform more than twenty feet high with black cloth draped on all four sides and a staircase leading to the top. A squadron of soldiers stood at attention while a growing crowd of people gathered on the periphery to watch.

Upon alighting from their carriages, the prisoners, barely recognizable to one another after eight months in prison, exchanged glad—if muted—greetings. No one had a clear idea as to what was going on, but there was an excitement in the air. It seemed that some decision concerning their fate had at long last been reached.

Just then, an officer on horseback rode up to the group and ordered them to line up by name. After the roll call, an Orthodox priest stepped forward and told them that they would bear the just decision of their case.

Holding a crucifix in front of him, the priest led the men past the waiting soldiers and up the staircase to the platform.

Fyodor and the others were divided into groups and ordered to remove their headgear while their sentences were read. To their horror and dismay, one after the other was condemned to execution by firing squad! They were directed to turn their gaze to three stakes planted firmly in the ground nearby. There they would be tied, three at a time, and shot. The priest now conveniently reappeared, inviting each man to make a public confession of sins. No one took him up on the offer, but all of them—even the diehard atheists—kissed the proffered cross.

The first three to be led away included the group's leader, Mikhail Petrashevsky. They were taken back down the staircase and tied to the stakes. Hoods were placed over their heads to prevent them from looking at their executioners, though Petrashevsky refused to have his head covered. Fyodor, next in line with two others, watched from the scaffolding. Years later, he described feeling in that moment "only a mystic terror . . . completely dominated by the thought that in perhaps five minutes, I would be going to another, unknown life."[2]

"Ready!" rang out the commanding officer's voice. "Aim!" Fyodor drew his breath, anticipating the awful, final command and volley of gunfire. Seconds passed in unbearable silence until, abruptly, a drum roll commenced, and the soldiers lowered their guns with a synchronized clatter. A horse-drawn carriage rolled into the square and a state official emerged. He announced that the emperor had granted the prisoners a reprieve; the entire ordeal had been a mock execution staged by Tsar Nicholas to teach the prisoners a lesson in loyalty.

At this news, a man named Nikolay Grigoryev snapped. He had shown signs of mental instability in prison and now went over the edge. He would never recover. The cruel spectacle continued as Petrashevsky was shackled in heavy leg irons, dragged unceremoniously to a rough wooden cart, and exiled for life to Siberia. The other prisoners were returned to the fortress.

Fyodor's actual sentence was handed down: four years of hard labor followed by military service for an indeterminate time as a private in the Russian army. Day and night, Fyodor paced his cell, singing at the top of his lungs and thanking God for the gift of life—a gift that had never before seemed so precious. He took time to write a letter to his older brother, Mikhail.

In four years my lot will be easier. I will be a soldier, and
that's different from being a convict . . . Will my body
hold out? I don't know. I am leaving in ill health, but
never before have I felt welling up in me such abundant
and healthy reserves of spiritual life as I do now.[3]

The following day, Fyodor was allowed to meet his brother
briefly and bid him farewell. Mikhail wept bitterly at the
parting, but Fyodor was calm, letting his brother know how
he viewed his banishment to *katorga* (prison camp). "Misha,
there are not wild beasts in *katorga* but people, perhaps better than I am, perhaps worthier than I am."[4]

He and his fellow prisoners, all of them shackled in leg
irons, left the Peter and Paul Fortress in uncovered wagons
and headed east toward the Siberian steppes. They crossed
the Ural Mountains in a driving snowstorm, then wended
their way to the fortress city of Tobolsk, a transshipment
point for prison camps around Siberia. Fyodor and another
prisoner named Sergei Durov were assigned to *katorga* in
Omsk.

The day before Fyodor and Durov's departure from Tobolsk, three Decembrist wives arranged to visit them. The
appellation of "Decembrist" was a badge of honor for these
women, who for the last twenty-five years had lived volun-
tarily in exile with their husbands. They were well known
for their deeds of charity in and around Tobolsk and for
taking every opportunity to encourage and console newly
arrived exiles.

"The meeting lasted an hour," Fyodor wrote later in *A
Writer's Diary*. "They blessed us as we entered on a new life,
made the sign of the cross, and gave us a New Testament—the

only book allowed in prison. It lay under my pillow during four years of penal servitude. I read it sometimes, and read it to others. With it, I taught one convict to read."[5] Another gift lay inside the testament's binding—ten rubles in banknotes to soften whatever blows lay ahead.

The next morning, Fyodor and Durov departed for Omsk, reaching their destination eleven days later. Fyodor, who was of Russian noble class, was in for a rude awakening among the mostly peasant prison population.

"Their hatred for the gentry passes all limits," he wrote in a letter to Mikhail, "and therefore they received us, the gentlemen, with hostility and malicious joy in our troubles."[6] It was a shocking revelation for Fyodor, who had pinned such high hopes on his utopian dreams of leading Russia's masses to lives of greater freedom.

In the same letter to his brother, Fyodor described the squalid living conditions in the camp barracks, a set of decaying and filthy wooden structures where prisoners slept on the bare floors while lice, fleas, and other insects scurried about.

It was in these conditions that Fyodor experienced his first epileptic seizures. In the cold and dark Siberian winters, when the convicts were locked in early and had to endure one another's company for hours on end, the scene was invariably one of "everything defiled and degraded."[7]

Fyodor saw it all. And he began to question his life's purpose.

"I reviewed all my past life," he wrote, "went over it all to the smallest detail . . . judged myself sternly and relentlessly."[8]

Reading between the lines, it was clear that Fyodor had come to the conclusion that he had failed as a "revolutionary" and that social change alone could never satisfy the deepest needs of the soul. Furthermore, the very people he felt called to lead—the Russian peasants—wanted nothing to do with him because of his elevated social class. Was there any possible way forward?

During Easter week, more than a year into his imprisonment at Omsk, Fyodor had a sudden and vivid recollection, bordering on the mystical, of a man remembered today as "the peasant Marey." Fyodor had known Marey in passing as one of the serfs who worked the property at Darovoe. He had given no thought to him for more than twenty years when suddenly—amid the degradation and filth of the prison barracks—a scene from his childhood came vividly to mind. He remembered with perfect detail being in the birch woods of Darovoe one summer afternoon when he heard someone calling out a warning that a wolf was nearby. Terrified, he ran into the nearest field where he encountered a serf named Marey, who took the trembling child under his arm and consoled him "like a mother." He assured Fyodor that all would be well, and making the sign of the cross over him, sent him home with the reassuring words that God's angels had him in sight.

Fyodor "awoke" from his reverie somehow a changed man, at peace with his fellow prisoners and alive with a palpable sense of God's presence and grace. From then on, the prison camp at Omsk ceased being the living hell he had first encountered.

And then there was that constant companion, the slender book given to him by the devout Decembrist women who had implored him to turn to God during his time of trial. How could Fyodor fail to be attracted to that book's central figure, the God-man to whom he had been introduced as a child?

The suffering servant who chose to empty himself of royal privilege to live among the earthly poor, whose acceptance of God's will led him to a Roman cross where he sacrificed his life for the sins of the world?

Slowly the truth began to permeate Fyodor's soul—all men are equally men; all men are made in the image of a loving God. The goal of universal brotherhood is not to be attained by class warfare but by mutual love and forgiveness. Here it was before him, rising up from the bowels of *katorga*—a hope that defied explanation.

Fyodor penned the following "credo" in a letter to Natalya Fonvizina, the Decembrist wife who had pressed the New Testament into his hand at Tobolsk, commending him to the love and care of God:

> God sends me moments of great tranquility, moments during which I love and find I am loved by others; and it was during such a moment that I formed within myself a symbol of faith in which all is clear and sacred for me. This symbol is very simple, and here is what it is: to believe that there is nothing more beautiful, more profound, more sympathetic, more reasonable, more courageous, and more perfect than Christ.[9]

Something beyond theology had gripped Fyodor's heart and mind. Something beyond debate. A Savior had revealed himself to Fyodor's soul and given him hope in the midst of despair.

Fyodor's prison sentence ran its course, and he was released in February 1854. "The fetters fell off," he wrote seven years later in *The House of the Dead*, referring to the heavy iron shackles he had worn day and night for four years.

I picked them up. I wanted to hold them in my hand, to look at them a final time. I seemed to already be wondering that they could have been on my feet just a minute before. "Well, with God's blessing, with God's blessing!" said the convicts in coarse, sudden voices in which there was also a note of pleasure. Yes, with God's blessing! Freedom, new life, resurrection from the dead.[10]

Fyodor would have liked nothing better at that point than to return to St. Petersburg to be reunited with his family and start life over again as a writer. But as a lowly private with the Siberian Seventh Line Battalion, he went instead to Kazakhstan, not far from the border with China. He knew that resurrecting his career as a writer would not be easy. He had been out of touch with the literary world for five years. Furthermore, under the terms of his sentence, he was forbidden to publish his writing.

Though it was against regulations, he asked Mikhail to send him all the books and periodicals he could get his hands on. Fyodor told his brother that the first book he intended to write would explore "the mission of Christianity in art." The working title was *Letters on Art*.

However, Fyodor's "day job" as a private in the army continued. In truth, he cut a forlorn figure—a once-promising literary has-been. To all appearances, his future held scant promise.

But he was not without his advocates, including influential members at the tsar's court, many of whom mounted a campaign, gradually at first, to ensure his rehabilitation. When Nicholas I died in 1855 and was succeeded by his more liberal-minded son, Alexander II, Fyodor's prospects began looking up. In May 1856, he was granted the right to publish, and in the autumn of that year was promoted to the rank of commissioned officer. The following year, his rights as a nobleman were restored, and he married a young widow named Marya Dmitrievna Isaeva. It was a brief, not altogether happy, marriage that ended with Marya's death from tuberculosis in 1864.

Fyodor remarried in 1867, and from that time until his death, his literary career flourished. His second wife, Anna, who had previously been his stenographer, nursed him through depression and epilepsy and gave him four children. She also became his publisher and managed his business affairs. It was during this time that he wrote *Crime and Punishment*, *The Idiot*, *Demons*, and *The Brothers Karamazov* (widely considered his greatest work). In a letter he wrote to explain his purpose for *The Brothers Karamazov*, he said, "I will force them to admit that a pure and ideal Christian is not an abstraction but a tangible, real possibility . . . and that it is in Christianity alone that the salvation of the Russian land from all her afflictions lies. I pray God that I may succeed."[11] He finished the epilogue to his magnum opus two months before he died.

As recorded by Anna in her memoirs, Fyodor had experienced pulmonary bleeding during the night of January 25, 1881. A doctor was sent for, but the bleeding continued and Fyodor lost consciousness. When he awakened, he had Anna send for a priest. He wanted to make his confession and receive Holy Communion.

Then on the morning of the twenty-seventh, after a good night's sleep, Fyodor awoke feeling "cheerful and healthy." The bleeding in his lungs had stopped and hope was thus revived that the worst had passed. The doctor predicted he'd be back to a normal routine in another week or so, and that night, Fyodor again slept soundly.

Early the next morning, Anna awoke to find Fyoder staring at her with wide-open eyes. "You know, Anna," he said, "I have not been sleeping for three hours now, and have been thinking all that time; and only now have I clearly realized that I shall die today."[12]

He then asked Anna to bring him his New Testament, the very same weather-beaten copy given to him by the Decembrist wives years before, which ever since had been his constant companion.

A few hours later, the children were called.

His daughter Lyubov (Aimee) recalled years later:

> He made us come into the room, and taking our little hands in his, he begged my mother to read the Parable of the Prodigal Son. He listened with his eyes closed, absorbed in his thoughts.
>
> "My children," he said in his feeble voice, "never forget what you have just heard. Have absolute faith in God and never despair of his pardon. I love you dearly, but my love is nothing compared to the love of God. Even if you should commit some dreadful crime, never despair of God. You are his children; humble yourselves before him, as before your father, implore his pardon, and he will rejoice over your repentance, as the father rejoiced over that of the prodigal son."[13]

A few hours passed, and Fyodor was gone. Gone to venture forth into that "other, unknown life."

Three days later an estimated fifty-thousand mourners walked through the streets of St. Petersburg. Countless people commented on how orderly the funeral procession was. One story tells of an elderly bystander, uninformed of Fyodor's death, who happened to ask one of the mourners who was being buried with such pomp and ceremony. The simple but telling reply was "an exiled convict." It was, perhaps, how Fyodor would have wanted to be remembered. It was while in *katorga*, after all, that he had experienced the mercy and grace of God and a sublime return to the faith of his childhood.

He was fifty-nine years old when he died and was buried in the Trinity Cemetery at the Alexander Nevsky Monastery. These words of Jesus from the Gospel of John are engraved on his tombstone: "Verily, verily, I say unto you, Except a corn of wheat fall into the ground and die, it abideth alone: but if it die, it bringeth forth much fruit" (John 12:24). Fyodor had quoted the same passage in his preface to *The Brothers Karamazov*.

Given the depth of Fyodor's Christian faith, it is curious that so many atheists and agnostics throughout history have admired him as greatly as they have. How can that be? The answer, perhaps, lies in his no-holds-barred exploration of the human psyche. He refused to shrink from a frank and candid examination of humankind in its fallen—that is to say, normal—condition. He gave full weight, with compelling insight and passion, to the arguments for human fortitude in the face of despair and seeming meaninglessness in life.

At the same time, he gave eloquent voice to the cries of the human heart to know God. It was his dream to unite the Russian people in love and Christian faith. That dream may yet be unrealized, but one thing is certain. Through his writings, Fyodor has given all the world lasting insights into the search for spiritual truth.

"I go to spread the tidings," he wrote in "The Dream of a Ridiculous Man" a few years before his death. "I want to spread the tidings—of what? Of the truth, for I have seen it, have seen it with my own eyes; have seen it in all its glory."[14]

Jean-Henri Dunant

I was a graduate student at Art Center College of Design in Pasadena, California, when I first learned of Jean-Henri Dunant. I had received the special opportunity to produce a public service TV spot for the Los Angeles chapter of the American Red Cross and decided to do something that would explore the origins of this great humanitarian organization.

My research led me to *A Memory of Solferino*, written in 1862 by Dunant, a Swiss businessman who had witnessed the aftermath of one of Europe's most bloody battles. Amid the carnage all around him, Henri found himself thrust into the front lines of a hastily-formed volunteer corps that attempted to meet the overwhelming needs of the wounded.

Something in the pages of his book, written in the first person, spoke to me of a Christ-inspired passion to make a saving difference in the world. Further research into his life revealed the story you are about to read.

IN 1859, LONDON'S BIG BEN first rang its massive chimes, Oregon became the thirty-third state in a union teetering on civil war, and construction began on the Suez Canal in Egypt. There were other, smaller stories to be told that year as well. Two thousand miles west of Suez in the French colony of Algeria, a young Swiss businessman was facing economic ruin. As far as he could tell, there was but one solution to his predicament—obtaining a personal audience with the French emperor, Napoleon III, and making a case for financial support from the royal family.

Jean-Henri Dunant, then thirty-one years old, had been living and working in northern Algeria for the previous six years, first as the representative of a Swiss bank, then later as president of an agribusiness firm that had acquired a vast landholding for cattle rearing and wheat farming. He had raised millions of Swiss francs to develop the enterprise and seemed poised for great success.

But his plan had one fundamental problem: Algeria was an arid land. Everything depended on ready access to water, and without waiting for authorization from local authorities, Henri had built a large water-powered mill to grind his wheat into flour. He had assumed that water rights would follow as a matter of course.

They did not.

Though French was his mother tongue, Henri's Swiss nationality worked against him. Jealous local officials—both French and Algerian—stubbornly denied him the water concessions he sought. With large sums of investors' money at stake, the young and zealous Henri secured letters of recommendation from high-ranking members of the French military and further hedged his bets by writing a personal tribute to Napoleon entitled *The Empire of Charlemagne Restored*. He bound the book in handsome leather to present to the emperor in person and set sail for Europe.

Meanwhile, Napoleon had declared war on Austria, which at the time was occupying most of northern Italy. Joining forces with Victor Emmanuel II, King of Sardinia and future king of a unified Italy, Napoleon and his allies won victories over the Austrians at Montebello and Palestro, followed by a third triumph at Magenta. As the Austrian army retreated eastward, Dunant, now in Italy and traveling by coach, adjusted his course to intercept Napoleon in the field with his troops.

On June 24, 1859, the decisive Battle of Solferino was fought. On one side stood the French and Sardinians numbering 140,000 men, with a roughly equal number of Austrian soldiers on the other side. The battle marked the last time in Europe that two opposing armies would fight under the direct command of their respective monarchs.

The first shots were fired a few hours before dawn, and the battle raged furiously across a front line stretching nine miles. Heavy rain fell late in the afternoon, followed by hail and lightning, and as the skies cleared, it was evident the French and their allies were victorious. The Austrians were in full retreat. Napoleon sent a celebratory telegram to his Empress Eugénie that read, "Great battle! Great victory!"

The toll of the battle was immense—forty thousand soldiers dead or wounded, houses demolished, farmland and orchards destroyed, thousands of horses and mules killed, the populace traumatized.

Henri, meanwhile, certain he had at last caught up with the Emperor Napoleon, rolled into Solferino that night by private coach, dressed nattily in a white linen suit to stay cool in the summer heat. To his chagrin, he learned that the emperor had already moved on. Due to the late hour, Henri decided to wait for morning to continue his pursuit. He didn't get much sleep, however, as he would record later in his classic memoir *A Memory of Solferino*.

"The stillness of the night was broken by . . . stifled sighs of anguish and suffering," he wrote. "Heartrending voices kept calling for help. Who could ever describe the agonies of that fearful night?"[1]

At daybreak, Henri approached the battlefield for a closer look. The terrible carnage of war was evident everywhere. The wounded were being rounded up haphazardly on the backs of mules or in rough village carts and transported to the neighboring town of Castiglione where every church, convent, public square, and house was being turned into a makeshift hospital.

"Some of the wounded had a stupefied look," Henri later wrote. Others "begged to be put out of their misery, and writhed with faces distorted in the grip of the death struggle . . . Bodies were piled by the hundreds in great common graves."[2]

The devastation Henri witnessed was shocking. While struggling to get a grip on his feelings, he weighed his options. It didn't take long for him to realize what he must do. The battle was over, the damage done, and he had not traveled this great distance to embroil himself in the affairs of warring nations. He had a mission to accomplish, a somber responsibility to investors. At least, that is what his head told him. The clear and emphatic voice of his heart, however, presented him with a much different course of action. To better understand the choice Henri made that fateful day in Solferino, surrounded by all the horrors of war, it is necessary to examine the influences of his youth.

Jean-Henri Dunant was raised in one of the leading families of hard-working and philanthropic Protestant Geneva during the time of the *Réveil*, a spiritual awakening in Switzerland marked by widespread religious fervor and works of public charity. His parents, Jean-Jacques Dunant and Anne-Antoinette Colladon, were active in helping the sick and poor as well as orphans and prison parolees, and their example was not lost on the impressionable Henri, their eldest child.

At eighteen, Henri joined the Geneva Society for Almsgiving, and the following summer, while hiking through the majestic Alps with two of his friends, he experienced a profound spiritual conversion. Not long after, he and his friends formed the "Thursday Association," which grew into a loose band of young men who met regularly to study the Bible and help the poor. For Henri, this meant spending much of his free time visiting prisons and doing social work. He soon developed strong ties with evangelical groups throughout Europe and the United States.

In 1855, Henri attended the inaugural meeting of the International YMCA in Paris, where he helped write the *Paris Basis*, which was ratified by YMCA branches worldwide. This charter document said in part that "the Young Men's Christian Association seeks to unite those young men who, regarding Jesus Christ as their God and Savior according to the Holy Scriptures, desire to be his disciples in their faith and in their life, and to associate their efforts for the extension of his Kingdom amongst young men."[3]

Given his background, it was really no surprise that instead of stepping over the dead and dying in dogged pursuit of the French emperor, Henri decided to stay and serve the weak and wounded at Solferino. Knowing the Bible as well as he did, he must have remembered the parable of the Good Samaritan—that enduring story Jesus told of a "foreigner" who had stopped on his journey to care for a wounded man he did not know. In addition to whatever common decency and humanitarian concern were at work within him, a genuine Christian motivation surely prompted Henri to set out for nearby Castiglione.

The local people were generous and willing to help but needed direction badly. Henri, who had always been gifted at rallying people to a cause, focused on organizing volunteers to help the sick and injured. Even passing tourists were pressed into service!

Because he spoke French, Italian, and German fluently, Henri was able to moderate between all sides, ensuring—to the extent possible—that every soldier received attention regardless of nationality. "*Tutti fratelli!*" became the slogan of the townspeople. "All are brothers!" they cried, pouring their hearts and souls into caring for the wounded men.

And the organizer-in-chief certainly wasn't above the fray. Henri cleaned and dressed wounds, moistened parched lips with drinks of cold water, wrote letters home to the families of dying soldiers, and gave spiritual counsel when asked. The soldiers and townspeople alike referred to him as the "man in white" because of the linen suit he wore continually during those fearsome hours.

He worked for three consecutive days without sleep, and when he got his chance to make a personal appearance before Napoleon's civil attaché, instead of asking for water rights in Algeria, he appealed, successfully, for the release of the Austrian physicians who had been taken as prisoners of war so that they might also help care for the wounded at Castiglione.

It is fair to say that the course of Henri's life was forever changed in the wake of Solferino. What he experienced there—the suffering he witnessed and the gnawing sense of what could have been prevented if more thought had been paid in advance to the human cost of war—weighed on him heavily.

His business interests in Algeria continued to flounder, but that didn't seem to matter as much as before. In 1861, Henri sat down to write *A Memory of Solferino*, feeling throughout that he was "inspired by the breath of God." A force was at work in his life and thoughts. The seed of an idea that had been formulating for the previous two years was now finding expression in the last chapter of his book. He wrote, "Would it not be possible in time of peace and quiet to form relief societies for the purpose of having care given to the wounded in wartime by zealous, devoted and thoroughly qualified volunteers . . . Could not advantage be taken of a time of relative calm and quiet to investigate and try to solve a question of such immense and worldwide importance, both from the humane and Christian standpoint?"[4]

A Memory of Solferino was published in Geneva in 1862, and Henri's appeal for trained volunteers to help the wounded in wartime was readily accepted among Europe's ruling elite, including Napoleon III, who now took much interest in the young Swiss. The book also caught the attention of Geneva's leading citizens.

On February 7, 1863, the Geneva Society for Public Welfare appointed a committee of five, including Henri, to examine the possibility of putting his plan into action. They formed the International Committee for Relief of the Wounded and called for an international conference to consider the question of volunteer relief agencies. Henri, appointed as secretary of the group, crisscrossed the continent to rally support from heads of state.

Government representatives from throughout Europe gathered the following year in the "city of Calvin" and approved the 1864 Geneva Convention, which, among other things, designated medical personnel as "neutral" during wartime, required all sides in a conflict to respect the rights of prisoners of war, and adopted as its emblem the inverse of the Swiss flag—a red cross on a white background. Within three years, nine more nations had signed the Convention. Henri had transformed a personal idea into an international treaty.

However, this success did not come without devastating personal loss. For years Henri had neglected his business interests in pursuit of a humanitarian vision and in 1867 was forced to declare bankruptcy. Though he vowed to work hard to repay his debts, his reputation was irretrievably tarnished. The social outcry in Geneva led to calls for him to step down from the International Committee, and on August 25, 1868, he resigned as secretary and two weeks later was fully removed. That same year, his mother died. Henri had lost everything he held dear.

He moved to Paris, where he continued to be active in various humanitarian causes, including helping the French chapter of the Red Cross organize its response to the Franco-Prussian War. During this time he also advocated for a homeland for the Jews in Palestine, the abolition of slavery (which still persisted in many parts of the world), and the creation of a "universal library" to house recognized masterpieces of world literature that might promote better understanding among the nations. But none of these endeavors succeeded, and Henri became destitute. He withdrew from public life and wandered anonymously about Europe, often dining on a crust of bread and sleeping outdoors. To look more presentable, he often darkened his coat with ink and whitened his shirt collar with chalk. For the next twenty years, the "man in white" became an obscure and, finally, forgotten figure of history.

In July of 1887, Henri crossed into Switzerland from Germany, settling in the mountain village of Heiden. He was fifty-nine years old at the time, though he looked much older and suffered from eczema. When he checked into a local guesthouse, he had to wait in bed while his one set of clothes was washed and dried. It was during this stopover that he enjoyed a slight change of fortune. He had recently begun receiving a small monthly stipend from family members and found Heiden to his liking. He formed a friendship with a local doctor, Hermann Altherr, who treated his eczema and generally nursed him to health. He also befriended a young schoolmaster named Wilhelm Sonderegger and his wife, Susanna. After learning of Henri's background, Susanna founded a local branch of the Red Cross and asked Henri to serve as honorary president. He was pleased to accept the offer.

Henri continued to remain anonymous but was now able to enjoy some of life's simpler pleasures. He spent quiet hours reading the Bible and writing his memoirs. He also liked to stroll through the town's well-maintained public gardens, enjoying the splendid views of nearby Lake Constance. In April 1892, he moved to a residential hospital managed by Dr. Altherr and took up residence in a simply furnished ground floor room with a small terrace.

Who can say what people today would remember about Henri Dunant were it not for Swiss journalist Georg Baumberger, who happened to be traveling through Heiden when he met a kindly older man who turned out to be the founder of the Red Cross. Following an article Baumberger wrote, which was picked up by the Swiss newspapers, Henri's story spread to all of Europe. At the age of sixty-eight, he had been rediscovered, and the "hermit of Heiden" soon began receiving visits from government dignitaries and European royalty. In addition to other distinctions, he was awarded the Swiss Binet-Fendt Prize and received cash gifts from the Russian empress and other benefactors, which led to a marked improvement in his financial situation.

Henri's greatest honor came in 1901, when he was awarded (jointly with French pacifist Frédéric Passy) the first-ever Nobel Peace Prize for his role in founding the International Committee of the Red Cross. The ICRC's official congratulations is worth noting: "There is no man who more deserves this honour, for it was you, forty years ago, who set up the international organization for the relief of the wounded on the battlefield. Without you, the Red Cross, the supreme humanitarian achievement of the nineteenth century would probably have never been undertaken."[5]

Despite his return to the public eye, Henri continued to live quietly in Heiden and died there on October 30, 1910.

According to his nurses, his last words were: "Where has humanity gone?" It is not known if anyone standing at his bedside gave him an answer. We can have confidence, however, that Henri will one day hear these words from his heavenly Father:

> Come, you who are blessed by my Father; take your inheritance, the kingdom prepared for you since the creation of the world. For I was hungry and you gave me something to eat, I was thirsty and you gave me something to drink, I was a stranger and you invited me in, I needed clothes and you clothed me, I was sick and you looked after me, I was in prison and you came to visit me . . . Truly I tell you, whatever you did for one of the least of these brothers and sisters of mine, you did for me. (Matt. 25:34–36, 40)

Today's Red Cross, desiring perhaps to maintain a mostly secular image, does not present in its publicity materials much of the dimension of faith that influenced Henri from infancy and guided him throughout life. A handful of biographers even suggest that he forsook the Christian faith in his latter years, pointing to his dissatisfaction with organized religion and his refusal, as specified in his will, to be buried in a church ceremony. His plainspoken confession of Christ, however, which he repeated often in the last years of his life, provides a fuller context. "I am a disciple of Christ, as in the first century," he wrote. "Simply that."[6]

Joining faith and good works as he did, it is perhaps fitting to remember Henri by these words written to him in 1863 by a Dutch medical doctor commending him for his efforts on behalf of the Red Cross: "I really believe that in this cause you are carrying out God's work."[7]

The public service announcement I produced for the Los
Angeles chapter of the Red Cross won several local TV
advertising awards and even played at the headquar-
ters of the International Committee of the Red Cross in
Geneva. At the time we were only students scrambling
to make a small budget fit the needs of our production,
but we managed to re-create a scene from the Battle
of Solferino in the Angeles National Forest and depict
a young Henri, dressed in a white linen suit, attending to the wounded inside a historic downtown church
that doubled for the church at Castiglione. I succeeded
in bringing in a consultant from England, an expert
on nineteenth-century European military history, who
charged us nothing for his services. We got costumes
at a reduced rate from Paramount Studios and free use
of a thirty-five-millimeter Panavision movie camera with
prime lenses. Remember, we were film students!

I cast eager actors from Austria and Italy, and the
man we selected for the role of Henri was a French
actor looking for a break in Hollywood. When he learned
he had landed the part, he came to my apartment in
Glendale so we could talk. Toward the end of our conversation, I told him I would like him to read all four of
the Gospels because, as I said to him, "You must capture
the heart of a man who walked in the steps of Christ
and spent himself in service to others." He stared at me.
He had never read the Bible before. I handed him my
own copy of the New Testament. He tucked it inside
his jacket and rode off on his motorcycle. When the

day came for us to shoot in the church, he looked—and acted—every bit the part.

How does one do justice to the greatness and goodness of a man like Jean-Henri Dunant? We made a small contribution, perhaps, with our television commercial, which was called "The History of the Red Cross." I pray his inclusion in this book will do even more to maintain the Christian emphasis of his life's work.

ABRAHAM LINCOLN

It's a question most children are asked at some point in their early lives: "What do you want to be when you grow up?"

"I want to be a filling station attendant!" I chirped happily.

"A filling station attendant, Kip?" Kip was my nickname as a child. "Why on earth would you want to do that?"

"I like the smell the gas makes when it's being pumped into the car."

"I see. Is there anything else you'd like to be when you grow up?"

"Well, maybe a garbage man."

"A garbage man? Good heavens, Kip. You don't want to be a garbage man."

"Oh, but I do."

"And why is that?"

"Well, they get to ride on the back of the truck, just holding on with one hand, while it goes up and down the street." I proceeded to give a pantomimed demonstration. "Then they jump to the ground while the truck's still movin' along and jump back on the truck before it stops. That's gotta be a lotta fun!"

"I see. There's nothing else you'd like to be when you grow up?"

"Well, there is one other thing," I answered.

"What's that?"

"I'd like to be president of the United States."

I never could understand why this last response provoked laughter from the grown-ups. I was quite serious about it and quietly held the ambition for a number of years, letting it go in my mid to late twenties when I concluded that I had done too many "wrong things" in life to ever win such a high office. But I still believe— certainly, I want to believe—that a kind, down-to-earth, and unselfish person can be elected to lead their country toward a better future.

Someone like Abraham Lincoln, for instance, the sixteenth president of the United States.

THE YEAR WAS 1849 IN LEXINGTON, KENTUCKY. Robert S. Todd, distinguished native son, lay dead of cholera, and his son-in-law, a successful attorney from Illinois, was charged with sorting out his tangled legal estate. First impressions of the son-in-law were not impressive. He was rather homely looking, tall and gangly, with unkempt hair and large, coarse hands that looked better fit for wielding an axe or ploughshare than for paging through a law book. In fact, during his lifetime he had received no more than twelve or so months of formal education.

But appearances can be deceiving.

For one thing, the tall prairie lawyer had a thorough knowledge of the law. And he loved to read. While in Lexington, he often escaped to the quiet seclusion of Mr. Todd's library, happy and content spending hours among the hundreds of titles that lined the shelves. He may not have looked the part of a well-heeled bibliophile, but Abraham Lincoln was in fact a well-educated man. Self-educated might be a more fitting description.

His mother, Nancy Hanks, was his first teacher, and her influence on him was indelible. She taught him how to read from the Bible and to memorize passages of Scripture. Among Abraham's earliest memories were those of his mother teaching him the Ten Commandments and sweetly singing hymns inside the log cabin where they lived. As a grown-up, he would say of her, "All I am, and ever hope to be, I owe to my angel mother."[1]

When Abraham was nine years old, Nancy came down with milk sickness, a common and often fatal malady contracted by drinking milk from farm cows that had eaten white snakeroot plant containing the toxin tremetol. Nancy's dying words to her only son were to be kind to his father and sister, to live as she had taught him, and "to love [his] Heavenly Father and keep his commandments."[2]

Nancy's place in the home was filled a year later by a loving stepmother, Sarah Bush Johnston, who noted Abraham's precocious intellect and further encouraged his love of reading. By the time he was a young teen, Abraham had begged or borrowed "every book he had ever heard of in that county for a circuit of fifty miles."[3] *The Pilgrim's Progress*, *Robinson Crusoe*, *Aesop's Fables*, *The Life of George Washington*, and *The Autobiography of Benjamin Franklin* were just some of the titles Abraham read many times over whenever he managed a break from the rigors of frontier life.

When Abraham turned twenty-one, he set out on his own, journeying to New Salem, Illinois, where he found a job as a clerk in a small general store. Here he earned the moniker "Honest Abe" for his scrupulous dealings with customers, once walking six miles to refund a woman's inadvertent overpayment of a few cents. In time he became a land surveyor and the town's postmaster, joined the local debating society, and delved into politics, all the while continuing his informal education.

No book was safe from his grasp. Mentor Graham, the village schoolmaster, helped him work his way through *A Compendium of English Grammar*, while other friends loaned him books on mathematics, the classics of Greece and Rome, and the plays of William Shakespeare. He soaked up the writings of liberal Enlightenment thinkers like Edward Gibbon, Thomas Paine, and the French philosopher Volney and prepared for a law career by reading (and rereading) William Blackstone's *Commentaries on the Laws of England*.

His quest for knowledge seemed insatiable, made quaint and whimsical by descriptions of him stretched out on the store's countertop reading a book, his head propped up by a bolt of calico, or reciting from memory whole pages from Shakespeare's plays while fishing with a friend. It all amounted to a college education (and then some) for Abraham, which was not uncommon on the American frontier,

where institutions of higher learning were few and far between and great men were often self-made.

But as King Solomon wrote in Ecclesiastes (a book Abraham would have known well, having read the Bible through
many times), there were potential pitfalls along the way. "In
much wisdom is much grief," the sage king had written centuries before, "and he who increases knowledge increases
sorrow" (Eccles. 1:18 NKJV).

It's fair to say that Abraham didn't see it that way. He was
ambitious and pragmatic and understood that knowledge is
power—power to unlock doors of opportunity otherwise
closed to someone of his humble origins. He was also true to
himself, following the path down which his inquisitive mind
led him, even if so doing meant being increasingly at odds
with mainstream views—particularly with regard to religion.

Indeed, many in town remarked that Abraham had become
an infidel, a label that didn't seem to bother him in the least.
Though he probably never reached a point of outright atheism (even the Enlightenment thinkers he so admired were,
after all, more often deists than unbelievers), Abraham did
become a frank skeptic of religion, specifically Christianity.

Another Bible passage, also attributed to King Solomon,
casts light on this period in Abraham's life. It's a promise,
cherished by Christian parents, that was undoubtedly close
to Nancy Lincoln's heart: "Train up a child in the way he
should go: and when he is old, he will not depart from it"
(Prov. 22:6).

When Abraham began his career in politics (he was elected
four times in succession to the Illinois House of Representatives beginning in 1834), he gradually tempered his antagonism toward Christianity. Some say he did so to gain broader

appeal among religious-minded voters—the majority of the electorate—and that may well be true. But, at the same time, he had begun rethinking his previous positions on the Christian faith. In conversation with a friend during this time, he described himself as being more of a doubting Thomas than anything else—a person who wanted to believe but needed supernatural help in overcoming his unbelief.

Also never far removed from his heart of hearts were the vivid memories of his angel mother. As he would attest later in life, "I remember my mother's prayers, and they have always followed me. They have clung to me all my life."[4]

After settling into his career as a lawyer, Abraham married Mary Todd in 1842, and the couple purchased a house in Springfield, Illinois. Forty weeks to the day following their marriage, Robert Todd Lincoln was born and Abraham became a family man.

It was a way of life he found agreeable. Left to his own devices, he could be despondent and depressed, while Mary was garrulous and refined, a social butterfly and regular church attender. Abraham loved Mary deeply and no doubt softened some of his views for her sake. He also loved children. The family began attending the Episcopalian church in Springfield, and the birth of a second son, Eddie, brought new reasons to celebrate. Abraham built up his law practice while maintaining ties to the local political scene. In 1847, he branched into national politics and was elected to the US House of Representatives as a congressman from Illinois.

His record in Washington was solid, if unremarkable. As a loyal Whig Party member, he supported national banking reforms and protective tariffs, while opposing the Mexican-American War and voting to abolish slavery in the District of Columbia. But after a year or so in the nation's capital, it was clear he was losing his taste for politics. What did it all mean after all? Where was the joy? What was his purpose?

Now here he was in Kentucky in the fall of 1849, sorting out his deceased father-in-law's estate. It was tedious work made bearable by the ready access he enjoyed to the quiet ambience of the library. Here at least he could be alone with his thoughts and indulge his thirst for knowledge.

It would be fair to say that at age forty, Abraham was experiencing something of a midlife crisis. His first and only term as a US congressman was behind him. What did the future hold, and what would his legacy be? And the larger questions that had so long preoccupied him: Is there a God? Does life have any meaning? To what end was the self-education he had so painstakingly acquired? As the Preacher wrote in Ecclesiastes, "People and animals share the same fate—both breathe and both must die. So people have no real advantage over the animals. How meaningless!" (Eccles. 3:19 NLT).

Just then a book title on one of the shelves caught his eye: *The Christian's Defence, Containing a Fair Statement, and Impartial Examination of the Leading Objections Urged by Infidels Against the Antiquity, Genuineness, Credibility and Inspiration of the Holy Scriptures; Enriched with Copious Extracts from Learned Authors.*

The longwinded title might have been off-putting to most people, but not to Abraham. He turned the volume over in his hands, recognizing the name of the author, Reverend James D. Smith of First Presbyterian Church in Springfield. Dr. Smith was a well-educated Scotsman, born in Glasgow, who had immigrated to the United States at twenty-one, eager to establish himself in business. He had been a confirmed religious skeptic who had enjoyed making fun of country preachers at revivalist camp meetings until he was himself converted at a camp meeting in Indiana and became a revivalist Presbyterian! He had moved to Springfield earlier that year to assume the pastorate at First Presbyterian.

Abraham browsed the pages of the book. It was a two-volume set, a scholarly defense of the Christian faith, which had its genesis in a series of debates Dr. Smith held in 1841 in Mississippi with a well-known atheist, C. G. Olmstead.

Abraham started reading the book in Lexington but stopped midway through when he returned to Springfield. What he had read of the book, however, made such an impression on him that he reached out immediately to close friend and fellow lawyer Thomas Lewis, whom he knew to be an elder at Dr. Smith's church. He asked Lewis to help him get a copy of the book, mentioning how he had read it about halfway through while in Lexington and was eager to get his own copy and finish reading it.

Mr. Lewis wasted no time introducing Abraham to Dr. Smith, who gave Abraham his own copy of the book and invited him to church the following Sunday. Abraham accepted the invitation. It was the beginning of a long and lasting friendship.

But ominous clouds were gathering on the horizon. Little Eddie became ill, his condition steadily worsening. Doctors had treated him initially for diphtheria, but now came a revised diagnosis: pulmonary tuberculosis, or as it was known at the time, "consumption," often a fatal illness, especially for children.

On a cold and rainy Friday morning, February 1, 1850, Mary Lincoln's cries were heard echoing through the family's house. Eddie had died during the night, a month shy of his fourth birthday.

It fell to Abraham to make the funeral arrangements. He discovered that Father Charles Dresser, Springfield's Episcopalian minister, was out of town and unable to officiate. So he turned to Dr. Smith, who the next day conducted Eddie's funeral at the Lincoln home, then walked alongside the casket the fourteen blocks to the cemetery. There Dr. Smith delivered a final eulogy.

In the weeks and months that followed, Eddie's heartbroken parents—Abraham especially—turned to Dr. Smith for comfort and counsel. "I found him very much depressed and downcast at the death of his son," Dr. Smith would recall several years later, "and without the consolation of the gospel. He gradually revealed the state of his mind and heart, and at last unbosomed his doubts and struggles and unrest of soul."[5]

Abraham was no stranger to death. He had lost his mother when he was nine, his older sister ten years after that, and now his own son. What was it Plutarch said? "Fate leads him who follows it, and drags him who resists?" Or as the Bible puts it, "Who can resist God's will? Are not our days on earth an evening shadow, a meaningless chasing after the wind?"[6]

During this dark and difficult time, Dr. Smith gave Abraham additional books to help dispel some of the gloom. He also encouraged Abraham to finish reading *The Christian's Defence*. It was the latter book in particular that continued to call Abraham's attention, laying out as it did in orderly fashion the positions on both sides of the debate as to the existence of God and the inspiration of God's Word.

"To the arguments on both sides, Mr. Lincoln gave a most patient, impartial, and searching investigation," recalled Dr. Smith. "To use his own language, he examined the arguments as a lawyer, who is anxious to reach the truth, investigates testimony. The result was the announcement by himself that the argument in favor of the divine authority and inspiration of the Scriptures was unanswerable."[7]

Had Abraham become a Christian? Dr. Smith was convinced that he had, not merely because of his reactions to reading the book, but because of many conversations the two men subsequently held. Abraham was mostly silent on the subject. His later words and actions, however, indicate that, at the very least, he had begun an earnest spiritual pilgrimage. As Mary noted years later, "From the time of the death of our little Edward, I believe my husband's heart was directed towards religion."[8]

Abraham and Mary began regularly attending First Presbyterian (Mary joined the church in 1852), and Abraham rented a family pew near the front of the sanctuary. His work as a circuit-riding lawyer often took him away from Springfield for weeks at a time, but on those Sundays when he was home, he faithfully attended church with his family, preferring to sit at the end of the pew so he could stretch his long legs into the aisle.

For as long as he remained in Springfield, Abraham contributed financially not only to First Presbyterian but also to several other churches in town. Dr. Smith referred to him as a "constant attendant" on his ministry and was himself a frequent visitor at the Lincoln home, where he enjoyed long and lively conversations on a variety of subjects.

Abraham, for his part, accepted a number of invitations from Dr. Smith to speak from the pulpit at First Presbyterian.

On one occasion, he addressed the Springfield Bible Society, closing with these words about the Bible: "It seems to me that nothing short of infinite wisdom could by any possibility have devised and given to man this excellent and perfect moral code. It is suited to men in all conditions of life, and includes all the duties they owe to their Creator, to themselves, and to their fellow man."[9]

So why didn't Abraham join First Presbyterian Church as Mary had done? Or any other church for that matter? He lived in an era in which church membership was all but obligatory for a self-professing Christian. Did he not know how people would perceive his failure to seek church membership? Did he not care? It was likely a matter of conscience. "I cannot without mental reservations assent to long and complicated creeds and catechisms," he said to a friend in 1846, referring to the denominational dos and don'ts of his day. "If the church would ask simply for assent to the Savior's statements of the substance of the law: 'Thou shalt love the Lord thy God with all thy heart, and with all thy soul and with all thy mind, and thy neighbor as thyself,' that church would I gladly unite with."[10]

Abraham became increasingly successful as an attorney, settling down to what must have seemed an idyllic life in Springfield. He was a decent, God-fearing man with a ready sense of humor and, when the need arose, a penchant for helping the underdog. He and Mary had another son, William Wallace ("Willie"), born a few days before Christmas 1850. Two and a half years later came Thomas, whom Abraham nicknamed "Tad" because he was as "wriggly as a tadpole" when a baby.

Had grief and troubles finally released their hold on the melancholic Abraham?

In the latter part of the decade, he again started dabbling in politics, helping launch the newly formed Republican Party in Illinois. At issue was the question of slavery and whether it should be allowed to spread into the western territories. Abraham was determined that it should not.

In 1858, during a series of stirring debates with incumbent Democratic senator Stephen Douglas, held as part of the Illinois senatorial race, Abraham gained the increasing attention of the American public. It was during this time that he delivered his famous "House Divided" speech, in which he referred to how the United States could not permanently remain part-slave and part-free; rather, it must become wholly one or the other. According to the election laws of the day, the Illinois state legislature, not the popular vote, determined the outcome of the Senate race, and Abraham lost to Senator Douglas. But Abraham's success on the stump led him to become the Republican Party's nominee for president in the 1860 election. The rival Democrats were splintered into various factions during the presidential contest, and by carrying the northern states, Abraham won the White House with a majority of the electoral votes. When word of his victory reached him in Springfield, he gently awakened a sleeping Mary to tell her, "We've been elected President."[11]

But it was a bittersweet victory, indeed, as the threat of civil war loomed large on the horizon. While Abraham was still in Springfield preparing for his inauguration and move to Washington, seven southern states seceded from the Union, forming the basis of the Confederate States of America. To what daunting task had he been called? Would he now be obliged as chief executive "to take arms against a sea of troubles," or was there, even at this late hour, some way he could avert impending disaster? As he confided at the time to Judge Joseph Gillespie, an old friend and legal colleague, it was as though he found himself in the Garden of Gethsemane, wrestling with God, his cup of bitterness full and overflowing (see Matt. 26:42).

When he left Springfield for Washington, DC, on a cold, snowy morning in February 1861, Abraham was seen off by a somber group of townspeople seeking to encourage him as best they could, empathizing with the challenges that lay ahead. He spoke extemporaneously to the gathering crowd from the rear platform of the train.

> My friends, no one, not in my situation, can appreciate my feeling of sadness at this parting . . . Here I have lived a quarter of a century and have passed from a young to an old man. Here my children have been born, and one is buried. I now leave not knowing when, or whether ever, I may return, with a task before me greater than that which rested upon Washington. Without the assistance of that Divine Being who ever attended him, I cannot succeed. With that assistance, I cannot fail. Trusting in Him, who can go with me and remain with you and be everywhere for good, let us confidently hope that all will yet be well. To his care commending you, as I hope in your prayers you will commend me, I bid you an affectionate farewell.[12]

Abraham made his way to Washington and delivered his inaugural address on March 4, 1861. As he neared the end of his speech, he declared in heartfelt words to all Americans, "We are not enemies but friends. We must not be enemies. Though passion may have strained, it must not break our bonds of affection."[13] But as every American schoolchild knows, the War between the States did, indeed, break out about a month later when Confederate forces shelled Fort Sumter near Charleston, South Carolina.

Many people on both sides of the conflict thought hostilities would end relatively quickly. Instead, the war dragged on for four years and more than a million lives were lost.

As commander in chief during wartime, Abraham was responsible for troop deployments and overall military strategy. Following the disastrous defeat of the Union army at the First Battle of Bull Run in July 1861, many people thought the best recourse for the North might be to sue for peace with the rebellious South. What would the president do? How would he handle the pressure?

James F. Murdock, a guest at the White House during the time, describes how he had been unable to sleep one night and was pacing the halls well after midnight when he heard a low murmuring coming from a private room near where the president slept. The door was open slightly, and he peered inside to see Abraham on his knees beside an open window, his face turned toward the night sky. Mr. Murdock heard Abraham praying in "tones pleading and sorrowful," asking God to grant him the wisdom he had once given Solomon. "I cannot guide the affairs of this nation without Thy help," he implored the Almighty. "I am poor and weak and sinful. Oh God, hear me and save this nation."[14]

But the trials would only deepen.

In 1862, while the war was still not going well for the North, Willie and Tad caught nasty colds. Tad made a slow recovery, but Willie's condition worsened. In all likelihood, the boys were suffering from typhoid fever, which they had contracted from contaminated drinking water. On February

20, at five o'clock in the afternoon, eleven-year-old Willie passed away. "My poor boy," lamented Abraham, looking down at his son's lifeless body. "He was too good for this earth. God has called him home. I know that he is much better off in heaven, but we loved him so." Then turning away, the words choking in his throat: "It is hard, hard to have him die!"[15]

For the next four days, Abraham produced no official correspondence from the White House. Mary was all but undone by the tragedy and could not attend the funeral. Abraham feared for her sanity and at times even questioned his own ability to continue as president. At intervals after Willie's death, he cloistered himself inside his office, his inconsolable weeping audible down the hallway. How could it be? His own dear Willie—so bright and lively, so tender of heart and full of affection! Only months before, he had happily told his family he wanted to be a minister when he grew up.

A deep solemnity came over Abraham in the wake of Willie's death. As the matchless Lincoln biographer Carl Sandburg explained, "Mr. Lincoln's views in relation to spiritual things seemed changed from that hour."[16]

Abraham talked at length with his pastor, Reverend Phineas Gurley of New York Presbyterian. Reverend Gurley had preached the sermon at Willie's funeral, and his ministry now continued as he helped Abraham shoulder the aching grief.

The president continued attending church on Sundays. His sorrow and weariness were palpable, as were the tender, almost delicate gestures he maintained—the gracious smile and nod of the head to his fellow congregants, the kindness and patience in his deep-set eyes.

During this time he made his way most Thursday evenings to the prayer meetings at New York Presbyterian, sitting just inside Pastor Gurley's office with the door ajar so as to listen and participate without being a distraction. And so in the midst of despair, with the outcome of the war still in doubt, Abraham somehow experienced God's grace to carry on.

It was during those dark days of 1862 that he entered into a solemn covenant with God, promising that he would set the slaves free should the Lord grant a decisive victory to the Northern armies that year. The victory came at Antietam on September 17, the bloodiest day of the Civil War. Following the battle, Abraham informed his cabinet of the oath he had taken earlier in the year. Then on New Year's Day in 1863, he issued the Emancipation Proclamation. The southern slaves were finally free.

The Battle of Gettysburg, an epic struggle fought in southern Pennsylvania over a period of three days, followed seven months later, ending in Confederate defeat and marking the beginning of the end for the South. Military historians have since debated ad nauseam about all the "ifs" at Gettysburg. About what would have happened if Lee had been victorious. Or if Jeb Stuart and his vaunted cavalry had not been missing in action during the first two days of the battle. Or if General Lee had not ordered Pickett's Charge. Or if Stonewall Jackson had still been alive.

There is another aspect to consider, however, a dimension beyond the purview of military science or historical interpretation. And that is the question of whether or not God is at all active in the affairs of nations. According to the deistic thinking Abraham once embraced, a supreme being started the grand show we call existence, then retired to some remote corner of the universe to do . . . well, no one knows what. However, the Abraham Lincoln of the Civil War did not believe this. By his own words, while president, he often got down on his knees in prayer during the darkest hours because he had become convinced there was no greater help to be found anywhere else. An eyewitness account recorded shortly after Gettysburg helps to confirm this.

Major General Daniel Sickles, commander of the Third Corps of the Union army, had been wounded on the second day of battle and his right leg amputated. He was recuperating in Washington, attended by Lieutenant Colonel James Rusling, when he received a surprise visit from President Lincoln. After an exchange of pleasantries, General Sickles asked if the president had been afraid during the recent battle—as so many others were rumored to have been—that Lee's army might triumph at Gettysburg and march on the capital. This was Abraham's response to the general, which Colonel Rusling detailed in his diary:

> Oppressed by the gravity of our affairs, I went into my room one day and locked the door and got down on my knees before Almighty God and prayed to him mightily for victory at Gettysburg . . . And I then and there made a solemn vow to Almighty God that if he would stand by our boys at Gettysburg, I would stand by him. And he did, and I will. And after that, I don't know how it was and I can't explain it, but soon a sweet comfort crept into my soul that things would go all right at Gettysburg, and this is why I had no fears about you.[17]

Abraham had faith in the God who rules nations, who decides military outcomes not by might or power but by his Spirit. The New Salem skeptic had become the praying president.

Four months later, Abraham delivered his immortal address at the consecration of the Soldiers' National Cemetery in Gettysburg, Pennsylvania, resolving that those who had died in battle should not have given their lives in vain, but rather, "This nation, under God, shall have a new birth of freedom and that government of the people, by the people, for the people shall not perish from the earth."[18]

A year after Gettysburg, Abraham was reelected to a second term as president by a wide margin. The Confederacy was teetering on defeat, and partisan voices clamored for a severe and exacting retribution that would cripple the South's ability to recover economically and humiliate them psychologically. Abraham could not share the acrimony. Instead, in a spirit of reconciliation, he called on the nation to bind up its wounds and work toward peace.

His second inaugural address, which he gave on March 4, 1865, reads almost like a chapter from the Bible, a book he had come to know so well. It was a brief address—only 701 words. In it he mentioned God fourteen times, quoted or referenced the Bible four times, and stressed the importance of prayer three times. He used the personal pronoun *I* only once.

Too bad his mother wasn't there. She would have been proud.

Five weeks later, on Palm Sunday, General Lee surrendered the Army of Northern Virginia to General Ulysses S. Grant at Appomattox Courthouse, and victory for the North was assured.

April 14, 1865 (Good Friday), dawned a beautiful spring day in the nation's capital. Everyone remarked how happy

Abraham looked that day. Senator James Harlan of Iowa stated that the last time he had seen Lincoln, he seemed almost "transfigured," and the "indescribable sadness" that had previously marked him "had been suddenly exchanged for an equally indescribable expression of serene joy, as if conscious that the great purpose of his life had been achieved."[19]

Abraham called his cabinet together that morning. He was decidedly upbeat and "more cheerful and happy than I had ever seen him," said War Secretary Edwin Stanton. "He rejoiced at the near prospect of a firm and durable peace at home and abroad."[20]

That afternoon, he and Mary took a carriage ride through town, just the two of them. Abraham spoke to her gently.

In the evening, they attended the play *Our American Cousin* at Ford's Theatre in Washington, DC. Abraham had no great interest in attending the show but had done so to humor his wife. After settling into their chairs in the presidential box, their intimacy from the afternoon continued as Abraham took Mary's hand in his and speculated about what they would do together after the war. "We will go abroad among strangers where I can rest," he told Mary. Then more specifically, "We will visit the Holy Land and see those places hallowed by the footsteps of the Savior . . . There is no place I so much desire to see as Jeru—"[21]

Before he had finished speaking the word *Jerusalem*, John Wilkes Booth fired a single shot from his .44-caliber Derringer pistol into the back of Abraham's head, just beside his left ear. Abraham slumped back, then forward, never regaining consciousness.

Booth jumped from the railing of the presidential box to the stage and fled the theater while a group of men, including several doctors, carried the mortally wounded Abraham to a boardinghouse across the street. They laid him on a bed—at an angle because he was too tall to fit otherwise—and began a vigil that would last for the next nine hours.

Attending physicians did all they could, but there was never any hope that Abraham could recover. At 7:22 a.m. on April 15, 1865, President Lincoln breathed his last. For nearly five minutes afterward, there was not a sound in the room. No one could speak. No one knew what to say or do. Secretary Stanton finally cleared his throat and asked Reverend Gurley if he would say a prayer. When the prayer was finished, followed by a chorus of *amens*, Secretary Stanton, with tears pouring down his face, spoke for all in the room when he said, "He now belongs to the angels."[22]

To borrow from Abraham's beloved Shakespeare, it seems fitting to quote Horatio's words from the end of *Hamlet*, "Good night, sweet prince, and flights of angels sing thee to thy rest."

Undoubtedly, Abraham Lincoln was a religious skeptic as a young man. Despite his mother's best efforts, he forsook the faith of his childhood. But as his mother no doubt understood (and prayed often), it was a faith to which, as he grew older, he would return.

In his terse second inaugural address, Abraham made reference to "the believers in a living God." Clearly, he had come to count himself among that number, and many witnesses would have attested to the fact. Why then the resistance to his life of faith?

The Russian novelist Leo Tolstoy described Abraham as a "Christ in miniature, a saint of humanity." Many in our secular age don't like to push too far in that direction. They're uncomfortable with a President Lincoln who was too heavenly minded, finding such a label incompatible with all the earthly good he did.

I have to wonder if we'll see a leader like him again in the public square. I wonder if society has become too sophisticated to allow a self-taught man to rise to the top or to trust a president who takes the Lord's counsel over the results of the latest opinion poll. But one should not abandon hope or grow weary. Perhaps there is currently a young child who wants to be president when they grow up. Perhaps they will be good and decent and kind and point this country back to the timeless truths of old. Perhaps we will see a new birth of freedom in this nation, under God. It's worth believing and hoping for.

Joseph Lister
and Louis Pasteur

"What's in a name?" asked Juliet of her paramour, Romeo, in William Shakespeare's classic play *Romeo and Juliet*. "A rose by any other name would smell as sweet." While that may be true of roses (and by extension, of Romeo), I draw the line in regard to Listerine. At least the Listerine of my childhood.

My mother insisted I use it as a panacea for various ailments, including dandruff and sore throat. Perhaps she was right. Mothers usually are. But that did not lessen my distaste for this antiseptic mouthwash with the mystical power to "kill germs by millions on contact." My one consolation was spitting it out—noisily and with great fanfare—after having swished it around in my mouth for several seconds.

But that was then.

I have since learned to be more grateful. Not for Listerine per se, but for the man who gave it its name—Joseph Lister, remembered today as the father of modern surgery. His introduction of antiseptic procedures in the operating room revolutionized surgery and has saved untold thousands of lives.

Listerine brings to mind another childhood memory associated with a highly recognizable name. I'm talking about pasteurized milk, for which we can thank Louis Pasteur, the great French chemist. Before pasteurization, beverages like raw milk spoiled easily, often causing sickness and death from illnesses like typhoid.

Today, Lister and Pasteur are remembered as great men of science, as they deserve to be. But there's another, largely untold, story surrounding their lives—they were also men of faith. "Posterity will one day laugh at the foolishness of modern materialistic philosophers," Pasteur once remarked. "The more I study nature, the more I stand amazed at the work of the Creator. I pray while I am engaged at my work in the laboratory."[1]

Likewise, Joseph Lister also turned to God in the operating room. When he was not yet thirty years old, he wrote the following in a letter to his sister after performing his first operation as lead surgeon: "I trust I may be enabled in the treatment of patients always to act with a single eye to their good, and therefore to the glory of our heavenly Father. If a man is able to act in this spirit, and is favored to feel something of the sustaining love of God in his work, truly the practice of surgery is a glorious occupation."[2]

Over the course of nearly thirty years, Joseph Lister and Louis Pasteur corresponded regularly, sharing their research findings and collaborating wherever possible to alleviate human suffering. In words that bring to mind the care and compassion demonstrated by the Good Samaritan, Pasteur once said, "One does not ask of one who suffers: What is your country and what is your religion? One merely says: You suffer, that is enough for me."[3]

JOSEPH LISTER HUNG HIS HEAD IN DESPAIR. He had done everything in his power to save the boy's life but had failed. Perhaps his grief was compounded by the knowledge that he and his wife, Agnes, would never be able to have children of their own.

"Don't take it so hard, Lister," said James Morton, a fellow surgeon at the Royal Infirmary of Glasgow. "Compound fractures often end this way. You know that."

It was a true enough statement but no consolation to Joseph. Surgery on the boy's leg—which had been badly damaged in a carriage accident—had gone perfectly well, but there was no controlling the sepsis, or infection, that followed. Joseph had spent years trying to solve the riddle of why wounds for which the skin is broken so often lead to the dreaded "hospital diseases" of gangrene, erysipelas, and pyemia. He had devoted untold hours of research to answering the question, only to come up empty-handed.

During the mid-nineteenth century, incongruous as it may seem to us today, the medical community had made no correlation between hospital hygiene and the spread of infectious disease. If a doctor washed his hands it was because they happened to be dirty. He had no awareness that his unwashed hands might also be deadly. Surgeons typically wore the same unwashed frock coat for years, the caked-on blood and gore a badge of honor. There was no concept of "sanitizing" surgical instruments, no masks for covering a doctor or nurse's nose and mouth. Hospital rooms were cleaned on average once a year, and if you needed surgery, there was a 50 percent chance you would never leave the hospital alive. As the saying went at the time, "The operation was successful, the patient died."

It all made for an intolerable situation that people at the time nevertheless resigned themselves to accept. But not Joseph Lister, for whom the existence of a problem argued the likelihood of a solution.

He came by his forthrightness honestly enough. Joseph Jackson Lister, Joseph's father, was a successful wine merchant, but his real passions in life were physics and optics. In 1830, he invented the achromatic microscope and early on encouraged his son's interests in zoology, botany, and microscopy. Young Joseph had the run of his family's estate in West Hampton, Essex (north of London), collecting and studying plant life, and dissecting animals and articulating their skeletons. While still a child, he boldly announced his intention to become a surgeon when he grew up.

In 1852, after obtaining his medical degree (with honors) from University College London, Joseph was made a fellow of the Royal College of Surgeons and in 1854 became first assistant to acclaimed Scottish surgeon James Syme at the Edinburgh Royal Infirmary. Mr. Syme (surgeons, as opposed to physicians, were called "Mr." back in the day) took a growing interest in his protégé, who demonstrated a keen and inquisitive mind, a meticulous approach to surgery, and a caring spirit for his patients. When Syme's daughter, Agnes, fell in love with the tall and handsome Englishman, the elder Scot found all the more reason to keep a watchful eye!

But now, at the age of thirty-eight, happily married to "Aggie" and tenured as Regius Professor of Systematic Surgery at the University of Glasgow, Joseph had begun to question whether, in fact, he had chosen the right profession after all. He had dedicated his life to the art of healing, yet his best efforts as a surgeon—and they were considerable—could be eradicated in a few hours by the ever-lurking specter of infection. "Anyone who could enable an open wound to behave like a closed one," he once told his Glasgow students "would be amongst the greatest benefactors of his age."[4]

Ironically, Joseph had instituted more stringent hygiene rules on his ward at the Royal Infirmary than was common at the time. These measures weren't enforced because of an understanding of how disease spread. They were more the by-products of Joseph's orderly nature and penchant for cleanliness. Yet when all was said and done, the infection rate on his ward was not greatly different from that of other wards.

The agonized plea of an early seventeenth-century Flemish chemist, Jan Baptista van Helmont, characterizes the frustration Joseph—and the entire medical profession at the time—must have felt.

O merciful God, how long will you be angry with man that you have not revealed one truth to your students in healing? Is this Moloch sacrifice pleasing to you, and is it your will that the lives of the poor, of widows and of children, be continually offered up to you in miserable torments and incurable diseases, or through the carelessness and ignorance of physicians?[5]

Truly, the world awaited a deliverer.

IN 1822, LOUIS PASTEUR, son of a tanner, was born in humble circumstances in Dôle, France. He showed no great aptitude for learning as a child, though he demonstrated a higher-than-average ability to draw and paint—so much so that his father, Jean-Joseph, a decorated sergeant major of the Napoleonic Wars, began to imagine him attending college one day.

Eventually, Louis's aptitude in science and mathematics bubbled to the surface, and after several years of studying and teaching at universities in Paris and Dijon, he became a professor of chemistry at the University of Strasbourg. There he met his wife, Marie Laurent, the daughter of the university rector. They married in 1849 and had five children together. Tragically, three of those children never reached adulthood—Jeanne and Cecile died of typhoid, Camille of tuberculosis.

Their deaths might have broken the will of a lesser man. But for Louis Pasteur, the cruel and untimely deaths of his daughters fueled a lifelong passion to alleviate human suffering. It also shaped the expression of his faith.

"I adhere to that which is inspired by the natural eternal sentiments one feels at the sickbed of a beloved child breathing her last. Something deep in our soul tells us that the universe is more than an arrangement of certain compounds in a mechanical equilibrium, arisen from the chaos of elements by a gradual action of Nature's forces."[6]

In 1854, Louis was appointed dean of the science faculty at Lille University and three years later became director of scientific studies at the École Normal Supériere in Paris. He became well known for his application of scientific principles to real-world needs and for his rigorous work ethic. "Chance favors the prepared mind," he once famously said. He would intervene to save the wine and silkworm industries of France from ruin, develop vaccines against anthrax and rabies, and create the science of microbiology, while disproving the theory of spontaneous generation (which held that living things can originate from lifeless matter).

He also contributed regularly to scientific journals, and one day in 1865, an article he had written on fermentation reached north to the Scottish port city of Glasgow.

A light rain created a soft patina on the cobblestoned streets of Glasgow as Dr. Thomas Anderson, professor of chemistry at Glasgow University, strode across the courtyard leading to Joseph Lister's office. He held in his hand the latest issue of *Comptes Rendus Hebdomadaires*, a scientific journal published weekly by the French Académie des Sciences. Aware of Joseph's busy schedule as both teacher and practicing surgeon, Dr. Anderson doubted he'd find anyone in, but to his delight Joseph met him at the door.

"*Braw*, Mr. Lister!" said Dr. Anderson in his forthright way. "Glad I found you! I've just read something of great

interest in this magazine, and I'd like your opinion on it."
Before Joseph could respond, Dr. Anderson continued. "Yes,
yes, I know you're a surgeon, not a chemist, but you're one
of the few people at this university interested in my line of
work, and well, sir, I'd like to know what you have to say
about it."

Joseph looked at Dr. Anderson with his grave, peaceful
eyes. "Is there one article in particular you'd like me to read?"
he asked politely.

"This one," Dr. Anderson replied emphatically, poking
at the magazine. "This one by Louis Pasteur. It's about his
research with fermentation, and I think there's something in
it that will speak to you. Quite sure of it, in fact."

His curiosity piqued, Joseph took the magazine. "I will
do so," he said softly.

"*Braw!*" said Dr. Anderson, allowing himself a smile and
walking off as energetically as he had arrived.

Later that night, Joseph sat down by his fireplace at home
to read the magazine. He was fluent in French and became
immediately engrossed in Pasteur's article. Aggie knew better
than to bother him at times like this. But when he was still
bent over the magazine at two o'clock in the morning, no
longer reading but somewhere far away—lost in thought—
she took a different tack.

"Joseph, dear. You really should get some sleep, even a few
hours. You have a full day tomorrow. Come to bed now, love."
Joseph didn't answer but instead gripped Aggie's hands, a
strange light in his eyes.

"The apostle Paul," he said to her. "Do you remember?"
Aggie stared at him.

"When the scales fell from his eyes, remember?"

150

"The scales? What on earth?" Alarmed, Aggie put her hand to Joseph's forehead to see if he was running a fever.

"It's perfectly clear to me now," said Joseph, turning to the magazine. "It's all here. A French chemist, Louis Pasteur. He's demonstrated that sour wine, sour milk—it comes about as the result of microbes."

"Microbes?"

"Minute, living organisms. Pasteur calls them germs. They can be seen only under a microscope. I've seen them myself when I've examined diseased human tissue. I just didn't know what to call them. These germs are in the air all around us, Aggie—all the time. They cause fermentation in wine. But they also cause wine to spoil."

Aggie could only shake her head. "Dear husband, what does all this have to do with your work as a surgeon?"

"Don't you see, Aggie? These 'germs' in the air are the agents that carry disease. When a person is healthy, the germs can do little harm because the skin acts as a shield, keeping them at bay. But when they get into an open wound, they produce the poison we call gangrene and the other hospital diseases. Now I know what the enemy looks like, Aggie. Now I know who we're fighting!"

Over the next weeks and months, Joseph successfully replicated Louis Pasteur's experiments in his laboratory and before his students at the university. After learning that carbolic acid, a tar derivative, was being used in the city of Carlisle to safely kill parasites found in sewage, Joseph began using a formulation of diluted carbolic acid to wash his surgical instruments, his hands, and the bandages hospital workers applied to patients' wounds. He instructed the surgeons on his wards to do the same and to spray the operating rooms with a carbolic acid mixture to kill airborne germs. The results were near immediate and without precedent. His wards at the Royal Infirmary became free of sepsis almost overnight and stayed free for months on end.

Astonishingly, many people resisted his changes, including those in the medical community who claimed that his emphasis on combating hospital diseases was a waste of time and money. Nurses resented the extra work that accompanied his new hygiene standards, while many doctors chafed at the implication that their failure to implement his antiseptic measures made them complicit in patients' deaths or amputations. A few even vilified Joseph on religious grounds, asserting that he was interfering with God's will by trying to bring healing to people whom God had ordained to suffer. Raised in the Quaker tradition and averse to quarreling and confrontation, Joseph preferred to keep his thoughts to himself and concentrate on his work and research.

Louis Pasteur also suffered scorn from the medical establishment, primarily because—as a chemist—he was not a member of the medical fraternity. The "Pontiff of Microbiolatry," scoffed one critic, dismissing his germ theory of disease. Others referred disparagingly to Louis as "The Brewer" because of his research on fermentation. However, the criticism and vitriol did not slow down Louis. "I am on the verge of mysteries," he wrote in a letter to a friend, "and the veil is getting thinner and thinner."[7]

For his part, Joseph never tired of crediting Monsieur Pasteur with establishing the scientific basis for his own breakthroughs in antiseptic surgery and postoperative care.

The two men began a collegial correspondence, sharing details on their research and encouraging each other to boldly press on, especially as Louis's work branched into the field of immunology and he began developing vaccines against cholera and rabies.

Over time, both Joseph and Louis began receiving the recognition and honor they so richly deserved. In 1881, Louis received the prestigious Grand Croix of the Legion of Honor. His fame and success enabled him to raise the necessary funds to open the Pasteur Institute in 1887 for the prevention and treatment of infectious diseases. And in addition to Joseph's many distinctions, including numerous honorary university degrees, he became the personal surgeon to Queen Victoria, who knighted him in 1883.

Louis and Joseph met in person for the first time in 1878 when Joseph and Aggie attended a medical conference in Paris, where Joseph was the lecturer. There are no records of their conversation over lunch and dinner at the home of Dr. Nöel Guéneau de Mussy, Louis's close friend. We can only surmise that it must have included "shop talk" concerning their scientific research and sealed a growing friendship between the two men.

They would meet face-to-face on several later occasions, the final one being Louis's seventieth birthday jubilee on December 27, 1892. The Grand Amphithéâtre at the Sorbonne in Paris, which recently had been remodeled, was the venue for the standing-room-only crowd of three thousand people. The gathering included hundreds of students from the French *lycées* and universities, high-ranking government officials (including Sadi Carnot, France's president), foreign ambassadors and dignitaries, men of science and industry—and Joseph Lister, who was scheduled to speak on behalf of the Royal Society of London and the Royal Society of Edinburgh.

Normally Joseph would have found the undertaking stressful. He was shy by nature and sometimes stammered when speaking in public. But there were no impediments to his speech this day. Speaking in French, he extolled Louis for his painstaking research on fermentation, which had "pulled back the veil on infectious diseases," and for his lifesaving work developing various vaccines, in particular the rabies vaccine. Joseph also referenced the opposition Louis had faced early and often in his career, pointing out that his detractors had all grown silent in the face of his remarkable achievements. He concluded his speech simply enough by asserting that humanity was forever in Louis's debt.

And then, as Joseph stepped down from the podium to make way for the next speaker, he heard a familiar voice calling him from behind, "*Mon confrère . . . mon confrère.*" He turned to see the tear-streaked face of Louis, who, despite his frail health, had left his seat of honor to recognize *him*, Joseph Lister. With his hands outstretched toward his English friend and colleague, Louis beckoned Joseph to return to the dais. A buzz of excitement swept through the crowd as Joseph walked back up the steps and looked Louis in the eye. Overcome with emotion, he wept too. Spontaneous applause and loud shouts of "*Vive* Pasteur! *Vive* Lister!" echoed through the great hall as the two men embraced. It was an unforgettable privilege for those who were present to witness the scene.

But there was another sensibility in the room that day as well—a melancholy awareness that Louis Pasteur was not long for this world. In 1868, he had first suffered a stroke, which partially paralyzed his left side, causing him to drag his left foot. The stroke had done nothing to diminish his mental powers, but he had suffered additional strokes in the intervening years, and as a scientist accustomed to weighing the facts, Louis must have known the end was near. He acknowledged a spiritual dimension through it all. "I have the faith of a Breton peasant," he was once reported as having said, "and by the time I die I hope to have the faith of a Breton peasant's wife."[8]

Meanwhile, Joseph was enjoying a thriving practice and a teaching career at King's College in London. In the spring of 1893, he and Aggie went on holiday to Rapallo in northern Italy. After spending an afternoon in the countryside, enjoying a picnic and collecting wildflowers for later study (something the couple had enjoyed doing for many years), they made the long walk back to the inn where they were staying. Aggie was unusually quiet along the way and that night came down with chills and a spate of coughing. When Joseph checked her temperature the following morning, he discovered she was running a high fever. He went immediately for the village doctor, who confirmed Joseph's own diagnosis: Aggie had contracted pneumonia.

The end came quickly. Despite Joseph's best efforts to save her, Aggie died four days later.

How could it be? She had always been the *bonne vivante*, the garrulous, charismatic one who alone could draw Joseph out of his quiet reserve. Now she was gone, and Joseph was overcome by grief. He pressed on as best he could, fulfilling his commitments at King's College Hospital, but his private practice and laboratory experiments languished. At the encouragement of friends, he accepted the post of foreign secretary of the Royal Society, which seemed to revive his spirits somewhat, and in succeeding years became its president. But he generally avoided social gatherings, preferring instead the quiet beauty of the countryside and a deeper involvement in the Scottish Episcopal church to which he and Aggie had belonged during their thirty-seven years of marriage.

Across the English Channel, Louis spent time at his beloved institute, carrying on as best he could. But in November 1894, he suffered yet another debilitating stroke and was confined to bed rest at home under Marie's care and supervision.

Since he was not allowed outdoors during the winter months, people assumed the worst. But with the coming of spring, it seemed he might be on the mend. A small tent was erected for him in the new garden of the institute, and he would spend many afternoons under the shade of the young chestnut trees that had begun to flower. Old friends and acquaintances would visit him there, remarking on the keenness in his eyes, while acknowledging privately his physical decline.

On June 13, 1895, Louis walked down the steps of the Pasteur Institute for the last time, traveling with Marie by coach to Marnes-la-Coquette on the outskirts of Paris. After discovering the rabies vaccine in 1885, he had built a laboratory in this heavily wooded area and later an annex where he could live and work during the summer months. Close by the rustic house was a pasture with horses and a clearing surrounded by pines and purple beeches where he liked to sit during the warm afternoons.

He took particular delight in the frequent visits made by his grandchildren, and when it became too difficult for him to read on his own, he enjoyed having Marie or their daughter Marie-Louise read to him. Biographies, especially battlefield exploits from the time of Napoleon Bonaparte, had always interested him. "But he no longer looked with the same eyes on the glory of conquerors," wrote René Vallery-Radot, his son-in-law and early biographer. "The true guides of humanity now seemed to him to be those who gave devoted service, not those who ruled by might."[9] Men like St. Vincent de Paul—son of poor parents, tutor of a future cardinal, chaplain to convicts, and champion of abandoned children. Louis cherished the thought that he, too, might have done some good by the children of the world.

"The virtues of the gospel had been ever present to him," his son-in-law wrote. "Full of respect for the form of religion which had been that of his forefathers, he came to it simply and naturally for spiritual help in these last weeks of his life."[10]

Toward the end of September 1895, Louis became bedridden and, when offered a cup of milk, murmured weakly, "I cannot." He looked around the room at his family and colleagues with "an unspeakable expression of resignation, love and farewell." For another day "he remained motionless, his eyes closed, his body almost entirely paralyzed; one of his hands rested in that of Mme. Pasteur, the other held a crucifix."[11]

On the afternoon of September 28, 1895, Louis Pasteur passed peacefully into eternity.

We have no record of Joseph's reaction to the loss of his colleague and friend. Over the next nearly two decades, he would occupy numerous posts and receive many more honors and distinctions, including his elevation to the peerage in

1897. When asked in the same year Pasteur died to comment on faith from his perspective as a surgeon and scientist, he said, "I have no hesitation in saying that in my opinion there is no antagonism between the religion of Jesus Christ and any fact scientifically established."[12]

In June 1898, when he received the Freedom of Edinburgh award, he said, "As highly as I esteem the honor which you have conferred upon me, I regard all worldly distinctions as nothing in comparison with the hope that I may have been the means of reducing in some degree the sum of human misery."[13]

Lord Baron Joseph Lister died peacefully at his country home in Kent on February 10, 1912. At his funeral service in Westminster Abbey, a choir sang the following from George Frideric Handel's "Funeral Anthem for Queen Caroline," comprised of texts from the Old and New Testaments: "He delivered the poor that cried, the fatherless, and him that had none to help him. Kindness, meekness, and comfort were in his tongue. If there was any virtue and if there was any praise, he thought on these things. His body is buried in peace but his name liveth evermore."

I always struggled with science in school. Biology, chemistry, physics—they all occupied a niche in my mind akin to a mysterious black hole defying human under-standing (and interest). I remember being awakened one day in chemistry class by an eraser that Dr. Diehl had thrown at my head with pinpoint accuracy.

However, I am always excited to hear about men and women in the sciences who profess faith in God. I suppose that's because of the unspoken assumption in our day and age that "intelligent" people are not given to speculation on spiritual matters. As if faith and science cannot mix. But even a cursory glance at the honor roll of scientific greats reveals that many have professed faith in God. Galileo, Copernicus, Mendel, and Newton, to name a few and, in more recent times, numerous Nobel Prize winners have all affirmed strong belief in a creator. For example, consider this quote from Albert Einstein: "I want to know how God created this world. I am not interested in this or that phenomenon, in the spectrum of this or that element. I want to know his thoughts; the rest are details."[14]

It's funny, but that sounds an awful lot like something I might have said in Dr. Diehl's chemistry class. The truth is that I'll never have more than a rudimentary understanding of the medical and scientific breakthroughs achieved by people like Joseph Lister and Louis Pasteur. But my imagination happily runs wild at the thought of how they approached with reverence the question of the divine. I will always resonate with the depth of feeling that led Joseph Lister to treat his patients as his honored guests, to agonize over their suffering with tears, and to feel the "fearful responsibility" when introducing his hands "into such a piece of Divine mechanism as the human body."[15]

I also will be ever-inspired by the courage of Louis Pasteur, who battled through the deaths of his children and failing health, and, at great personal risk, extracted saliva from a living rabid dog to create a lifesaving vaccine.

These were not men who lived cold, detached lives in an austere science lab far removed from the warp and woof of life. They were individually gifted by God and uniquely motivated by his Spirit to work for the common good. All of us can be forever thankful for the tenacity they displayed, the discoveries they shared, and the indelible and life-changing contributions they made in this world.

CHIUNE SUGIHARA

Japan—the Land of the Rising Sun—has long intrigued me. My fascination probably began with the judo classes I took during my elementary school years. My instructor was the legendary Ed Maley, who had studied judo in Japan following World War II and was later stationed at MacDill Air Force Base near where I lived in Tampa, Florida.

Sensei Maley was short of stature and built like a steel-reinforced door. For at least two years of my life, if memory serves, he came to St. John's Parish Day School in the afternoons to teach a group of us boys the "way of gentleness" (the literal meaning of judo).

I took to it like a duck to water. I still remember some of the throwing techniques I learned. *Osotogari*, for example, favored my long legs. And I greatly enjoyed the art of breaking one's fall with a *zenpo kaiten* (forward roll). I took pride in my *judogi* (practice uniform), knowing that the color of my belt distinguished my rank. But

161

more than anything, I just plain enjoyed tussling with my friends.

An encourager by nature, Sensei Maley exuded tremendous enthusiasm and taught us much more than self-defense. We learned about courtesy, discipline, endurance, and even creativity. I moved up the ranks a bit, earning an orange belt and competing in a few tournaments. Who knows how far I might have gone? When I changed schools for junior high, my participation—though not my interest—in judo came to an end.

Then, at the age of eighteen I had an opportunity to visit Japan. I was enthralled by the juxtaposition of modernity with tradition, the beautiful landscaping and countryside, the inquisitiveness and industry of its people. I even fell in love with my tour guide.

When I went to Harvard University that fall, one of my electives was Japanese history and culture taught by Edwin O. Reischauer, a former ambassador to Japan and an expert in the field of Japanese studies. That same year I became a serious student of Japanese cinema and in my midtwenties began practicing Zen Buddhism.

I have learned a number of things about Japan and its history over the years, but until recently I never knew about one of its most heroic sons—Chiune Sugihara. His heroism is still largely unrecognized, but if ever anyone embodied the best and noblest aspects of Japanese culture and tradition, it would be this man.

IT WAS THE EARLY SPRING OF 1940, and the world was wondering if, perhaps, all the talk of a Second World War was just that—a lot of talk. Journalists at the time coined a derisive phrase for the lull in hostilities in Europe. They called it the "Phony War."

Not that there was anything to smirk about in Poland. In September of the previous year, Poland had been gutted in five weeks by a combined German and Soviet attack that gave rise to a mass exodus of Polish Jews into neighboring Lithuania—more specifically, the capital city of Kaunas, which for five centuries had been a hub of Jewish life and culture in Europe. Here at the confluence of the Neris and Nemunas Rivers, learned rabbis taught at dozens of *yeshivas* spread across town while the more secular-minded citizens had their choice of reading from the five Jewish newspapers published daily. Well-established artists, writers, business entrepreneurs, doctors, and lawyers all called Kaunas home. It seemed impossible to believe that such a vibrant community, now swollen by thousands of refugees, could be in danger of annihilation.

But it most surely was.

In April and May of 1940, the world discovered that the "Phony War" was deadly real. Norway, the Netherlands, Luxembourg, and Belgium fell like dominoes before the German *blitzkrieg,* and by early June, France was on the verge of capitulation. Panic began to overtake the Jews in Kaunas. Some in the community counseled patience, a wait-and-see attitude, while others saw the handwriting on the wall and began looking for a way out. But where would they go? Who would have them?

Returning west through Nazi-occupied Europe was out of the question, everyone knew that. Travel eastward was likewise improbable. The Soviet Union had no love for the Jews.

Nor were traditional allies of the Jewish people much help. The United States was carefully keeping its distance in the conflict, still toeing an official line of neutrality, while Great Britain had its hands full preparing for what it knew would be its own day of reckoning with the German war machine.

Then on June 15, with an approving nod from Germany, the USSR launched its long-planned takeover of the Baltic states and "sovietized" Lithuania, Latvia, and Estonia. The Soviets seized private property, made mass arrests, and organized deportations. Overnight, Lithuanian Jews became Soviet citizens and subsequently lost any chance they previously might have had to leave their new "motherland."

Non-Lithuanian Jews, however, still had a slim chance of escape. Jan Zwartendijk, the sympathetic Dutch consul in Kaunas, had begun issuing visas to Polish Jews for travel to the far-off Dutch colonies of Curaçao and Surinam. But there was a catch. The only way to reach such distant lands was to cross the broad expanse of the Soviet Union on the Trans-Siberian Railway to the port city of Vladivostok, and from there to Japan. It seemed an impossible task. What could possibly compel the Soviets to "let God's people go"? And why would Japan, which was allied with Germany, look with favor on the despised Jews?

Enter Chiune Sugihara.

Born into a middle-class *samurai* family on January 1, 1900, Chiune was groomed by his parents and society to take a leading role in the modernization of Japan after centuries of isolation. Naturally enough, he would have been inculcated with the *samurai* ideals of honor, duty, and self-sacrifice. And while he would not have been expected to walk around in war regalia, he was certainly expected to be a *leader*.

His father, Kosui, cherished thoughts of Chiune becoming a medical doctor, but his handsome, athletic son had other ideas. He was drawn to the study of languages and loved learning about history. Disagreements between Chiune and his father reached the point that, when it came time for Chiune to apply to medical school, he deliberately failed his entrance exam by writing only his name on his test papers.

In the fall of 1918, on his own initiative, Chiune began attending Waseda University in Tokyo, majoring in English-language studies and working part-time as a longshoreman and tutor to pay for his education. While at Waseda, Chiune again broke with family tradition and entered *Yu Ai Gakusha* (Brotherly Love Learning Association), a Christian fraternity founded by a Baptist missionary to Japan named Harry Baxter Benninghoff.

But Chiune's time at Waseda would be short-lived. While struggling to support himself financially, he answered a classified ad for candidates interested in a diplomatic career with the Japanese Foreign Ministry. He passed the difficult entrance exam and was assigned to the national language institute in Harbin, China, near the border with the Soviet Union.

While at the institute, Chiune became fluent in Russian and German and went on to graduate with honors. In the years following, he taught at the *gakuin* (academy) part-time and worked his way through the diplomatic ranks to become vice minister of foreign affairs. While serving in this capacity, he negotiated Japan's purchase of the North Manchurian Railroad from the Soviet Union in 1932 on terms highly favorable to the Japanese government. Chiune's success subsequently earned him a spot in line to become Japan's minister of foreign affairs for all of Manchuria.

Cosmopolitan Harbin was also where Chiune fell in love. Her name was Klaudia Semionovna Apollonova, a Russian immigrant. Many Russians had sought refuge in Harbin following the Russian Revolution, and Chiune embraced her Eastern Orthodox faith prior to their marriage in December 1924. He was also baptized in the church, taking on the Russian name of Sergei Pavelovich ("Sergei" because it sounded similar to "Sugihara," and "Pavel" because it was the name of the priest who had performed the wedding ceremony).

By this time, Chiune self-identified as Russian almost as much as Japanese and became thoroughly knowledgeable of the Russian language and culture. Klaudia, however, did not want children (she had two abortions without telling Chiune), and the marriage ended in divorce in 1934.

Still, Chiune's faith in Christ remained intact. And his conscience seems never to have lagged too far behind his actions. Deeply troubled by Japan's cruel treatment of the Chinese people under its rule in Manchuria, he resigned his post in protest and was reassigned to Tokyo.

Shortly thereafter he married a Japanese girl named Yukiko, who embraced his Orthodox faith and adopted the name Maria. They had two children by March 1939, when he was sent to Kaunas, Lithuania, to run the newly opened Japanese consulate. (In reality, his main purpose for being there was to monitor German and Russian military maneuvers in the area.)

Life in Kaunas was pleasant for the growing Sugihara family. They lived in a spacious, well-appointed home in a quiet residential neighborhood with the consular office located in the half-basement at the front of the house. The war enveloping Europe, while threatening, still seemed far enough away to allow them to enjoy family outings in the countryside and the endless soirees of the international diplomatic community.

But one could see ominous portents of what lay ahead. The Sugiharas learned firsthand from acquaintances in Kaunas's Jewish community of the atrocities being committed by SS-run killing squads (*einsatzgruppen*), which were "Jew hunting" in newly conquered Poland, murdering thousands of innocent civilians and destroying Jewish businesses and synagogues.

It's important to remember that during Hitler's awful rise, the Japanese, by and large, did not share the anti-Semitism of their Axis allies (and Westerners in general). To the contrary, their view of the Jewish people was mostly favorable because of the Jews' reputation as cultured, intellectual, and business-minded people. Plus, it was no secret that Asians as well as Jews were often the target of European racial prejudice. Hitler may have bent the Nuremburg Laws to allow for the Japanese to be deemed "honorary Aryans," but in more private discussions, he dismissed them contemptuously as "lacquered half-monkeys who must be made to feel the knout [whip]."[1]

Then came July 27, 1940. A day that changed everything in the Sugihara household.

Early that Saturday morning, a crowd of people began gathering outside the gate surrounding the Japanese consulate. It was a noisy, desperate throng that grew louder and more numerous by the minute. Several of the younger men began climbing the gate but were pushed back by security personnel. Chiune went outside and talked with leaders of the group and discovered they were mostly Polish Jews looking for a way out of Lithuania. Many of them carried visas provided by the Dutch consulate but needed additional transit visas through the Soviet Union and Japan to ensure their escape.

Chiune explained that he could issue a few visas under his own authority, but providing transit visas for hundreds of people would require the Japanese government's permission. He asked the Jewish leaders to give him time to consider their request and retired inside the house. His wife, Yukiko, described what happened next.

"My husband came up to the second floor with a worried look. He sat at the table in silence and drank some coffee. He waited until the outside grew silent. Then he stood up and went to the window and looked outside; so did I."[2]

The scene below broke their hearts. The crowd was dispersing slowly. Worried-looking parents held tightly to their children's hands, their eyes pleading for mercy as they caught sight of the Sugiharas in the bedroom window. Even Chiune's children were affected by the sight. They asked their father if he was going to help the "poor little children" who looked so desperate and forlorn. The answer, of course, was yes. He would do all he could. What did the old *samurai* maxim say? "Even a hunter cannot kill the bird that flies to him for refuge."

But there were ramifications to consider. Issuing visas to Polish Jews would likely be deemed a hostile act toward Nazi Germany. With the Japanese and German governments cozying up to each other for military and political purposes, Chiune knew that any request to issue visas to the Jews would not be well received by the home office in Tokyo.

Also, what could he hope to accomplish in the few short days he and his family had remaining in Kaunas? Lithuania was no longer a sovereign nation. It had been absorbed into the USSR, and the Japanese consulate, along with all the foreign consulates in Kaunas, had been ordered to close operations by the end of the month.

It was a sleepless night for Chiune. Ordinarily, he liked to tell his sons a bedtime story. But not this evening.

"That night he didn't talk to the children," Yukiko recounted. "It seemed that many cares for the Jewish people occupied his mind. Then Lamentations, a book of the Old Testament, suddenly came to my mind, which was written by Jeremiah, a prophet and poet, when he witnessed the fall of Jerusalem brought about by the Babylonian Army. My husband and I are Christians of the Greek [Orthodox] Church, so we desired earnestly to help the Jews."[3]

The next morning, Chiune sent the following cable to the Foreign Ministry: "Hundreds of Jewish people have come to the consulate here in Kaunas seeking transit visas. They are suffering greatly. As a fellow human being, I cannot refuse their requests. Please permit me to issue visas to them."[4]

He quickly received an answer from his superiors in Tokyo. There would be no transit visas for the Jews. Meanwhile, the crowd at the gate had grown larger. Chiune asked to speak with the group's leaders again, breaking the news to them as gently as he could.

On July 30, he again asked permission to grant visas and was again denied, this time on the dubious grounds that the presence of so many foreigners on Japanese soil would jeopardize public security.

Chiune debated making a third and final appeal. Was it worth the trouble, knowing where his government stood on the matter? What could he hope to accomplish with yet another request? Wasn't he endangering his family and courting personal disaster? Perhaps it really was time to leave Kaunas. After all, the other diplomats had all left town or were in the process of leaving. Only he and the Dutch consul remained. But the choice was not so simple. At least not for Chiune.

"I have to do something," he explained to Yukiko as he continued to weigh his decision. "A young man comes into my home for protection. Is he dangerous? No. Is he a spy? No. Is he a traitor? No. He's just a Jewish teenager who wants to live."[5]

Chiune sent a third cable to Tokyo requesting permission to issue visas. When the answer was again no, Chiune almost felt relief. Though he knew it would likely cost him his diplomatic career, even put his life at risk, he was now resolute. With Yukiko's full support, he made the decision to write the visas on his own authority. "I may have to disobey my government," he told Yukiko. "But if I don't, I will be disobeying God."[6]

Chiune paid a hurried visit to the Soviet embassy. His familiarity with the Russian culture and ability to speak the language seemed to open all the right doors. He hurried home to Yukiko with the good news. The Soviets had agreed to issue visas for the Jews to travel on the Trans-Siberian Railway all the way to Vladivostok.

Now it was time to get to work.

For the next twenty-nine days, Chiune worked tirelessly to issue transit visas for the waiting refugees. His original goal had been to write three hundred visas a day, but that quickly proved unrealistic. The appropriate consular forms were in short supply, and Chiune had to write everything by hand.

Yukiko was willing to help him with the required information, but he wouldn't allow her to participate directly. Were he to be arrested for his actions, he did not want anyone else to share the blame.

The days were long and laborious. He never stopped to eat lunch, and when he fell into bed at night, Yukiko routinely massaged his arm and hand, which was stiff and sore from the unrelenting pace of the day's work.

Initially, he followed the established protocol of numbering the visas and keeping a list of names, but after a few days, he simply issued visas to everyone who appeared before him. With a twinkle in his tired eyes, he taught the refugees how to say *Banzai Nippon!* ("Long live Japan!") in preparation for that future moment when they would likely face Japanese border guards and need special consideration. Others recall him speaking to them in Spanish as he handed them their ticket to freedom. "*Vaya con Dios,*" he said. Everyone noted his warm, friendly smile and kind demeanor.

Years later, looking back on those days, Chiune said,

> You want to know about my motivation, don't you? Well, it is the kind of sentiment anyone would have when he actually sees refugees face-to-face, begging with tears in their eyes. He just cannot help but sympathize with them. Among them were the elderly and women. They were so desperate that they went so far as to kiss my shoes . . . It was with the spirit of humanity and neighborly friendship that I ventured to do what I did.[7]

Nonetheless, Chiune's window of opportunity was growing short. The Foreign Ministry had originally ordered him to close the consulate on August 2, but Chiune had managed to obtain an extension from the Soviet authorities to keep it open until the end of the month. Then on August 28 he received an urgent telegram from Tokyo insisting that he close the consulate without further delay and leave for Berlin.

He had done what he could.

He sent the consular seal and important documents by diplomatic pouch to Berlin and moved with his family to a hotel at the center of Kaunas for three days of rest. However, before he left the consulate, he posted a sign on the gate informing people of where he had gone. Though he could no longer issue visas, he could—and did—issue permission papers to the refugees who tracked him down at the hotel. These documents were used by many to escape Lithuania.

On September 1, as the family prepared to depart for the train station, Chiune bowed deeply to the refugees gathered in the hotel lobby and said, "Please forgive me. I cannot write anymore. I wish you the best."[8]

But with the heart of a true warrior, even at the train station Chiune continued to try to help the desperate refugees. As the train began to pull away, he leaned out the window and placed blank visas into the outstretched hands of people running alongside the moving train. The forms would be filled out later and used by even more refugees to escape the spreading net. One such refugee, a young man named Yehoshua Nishri, shouted, "Sempo Sugihara, we will never forget you. I'll see you again!"[9]

As the train platform in Kaunas faded from view, Hiroki looked solemnly at his father and asked if they were finally going to Berlin. Chiune nodded and fell instantly asleep.

Although he had flagrantly disobeyed orders, Chiune Sugihara was simply too valuable an asset for the Japanese government to call home. After a brief interval in Berlin, he was reassigned to Prague, then Königsberg in East Prussia, and finally to Bucharest, where he and his family were arrested by victorious Soviet troops in 1944. The Soviets held him under house arrest for eighteen months before allowing him to return to Japan in 1946.

Once he was back in Japan, Chiune was dismissed from his job and left to fend for himself. During the time he had issued visas in Kaunas, he had half-jokingly said that if he ever lost his job as a diplomat, he would use his ability to speak Russian to find other work. And so it was. For the next sixteen years, Chiune worked in relative obscurity as the manager of a Japanese export company with offices in Moscow.

The years passed, and it seemed that no one much remembered Chiune Sugihara and the lifesaving actions he had taken in Kaunas during those fleeting summer days of 1940. There is a saying, though, that the Jews never forget a promise. And nearly thirty years later, in 1968, Yehoshua Nishri, the same Jewish teenager who had waved good-bye to Chiune at the train station in Kaunas, finally succeeded (after many attempts) at finding "Sempo" Sugihara in Japan. At the time, Yehoshua was serving as economic attaché to the Israeli embassy in Tokyo. He still possessed the worn visa that Chiune had presented him all those years ago. When news of their joyful reunion spread, hundreds of other "Sugihara Survivors" came forward with stories of praise for the heroic Japanese consul. One of them was Zorach Warhaftig, who had been among the Jewish leaders with whom Chiune had met at the outset in Kaunas. With his Sugihara visa in hand, Zorach had made his way to the United States, and in 1947 to Palestine. He helped write Israel's Declaration of Independence and served as minister of religious affairs in Israel from 1962 to 1974. He described Chiune in these simple words: "Chiune Sugihara was an emissary of God."[10]

In 1985, just a year before his death, Chiune was recognized as "Righteous Among the Nations" by the Yad Vashem Martyrs Remembrance Authority in Jerusalem. All told, he issued 2,140 visas (many of which were for entire families). The Simon Wiesenthal Center estimates that six thousand people were saved because of Chiune Sugihara's intervention, while another forty thousand descendants are alive today because of his resolve to obey God rather than man.

Asian culture has much to admire. Amid my own search for truth and meaning during my midtwenties, I studied the world's major religions and settled on Taoism as the best philosophy I could hope to find. I admired its concepts of harmony with nature and its emphasis on being compassionate, moderate, and unassuming.

Then I read the Sermon on the Mount in an old King James Bible, and my life was forever changed. I had never bothered to explore Christianity because I thought it had nothing to offer me. But the words of Christ pierced my heart. I discerned quickly that "never man spake like this man" (John 7:46). The impression was so favorable, and at the same time so overwhelming, that I proceeded to read the entire Bible from cover to cover.

I would never suggest that Chiune's decision to disobey his government to save the Jews of Kaunas was quintessentially Christian. There are good people of all faiths (and no faith) in the world. Many of them are heroes. But given the cultural and historical context during which Chiune and Yukiko lived and worked, their courageous resolve under pressure was truly extraordinary. I cannot help but wonder if the apostle Peter's words in Acts 5:29 were echoing in Chiune's mind when he told Yukiko that he might be disobeying his government by issuing the visas to the Jews but that he would be disobeying God if he did not.

I pray with all my heart that I, too, will obey God rather than people, should I ever face a similar test.

CHARLES DICKENS

I was twelve or thirteen years old and can't say now how the book first came to me—whether I picked it up from my older brother's desk at home, or whether, in fact, it was required reading for my English class at Berkeley Prep School in Tampa, Florida. What I do remember—and vividly so—is how quickly I was drawn into the story. I could not put the book down, and when I finished it, I was undoubtedly a better person for having read it.

Great Expectations was my first introduction to the work of Charles Dickens. In subsequent years I would read *David Copperfield*, *Oliver Twist*, *A Christmas Carol*, and *A Tale of Two Cities*. Looking back, I can see how each of these literary gems presented a distinct Christian worldview, something my teachers at the time never talked about, choosing instead to focus on the writer's masterful use of character, dialogue, and story.

To be fair, Charles Dickens did not paint his characters or stories in obviously Christian terms. But what

I have come to learn is that his personal faith in Jesus Christ, together with his thorough understanding of the New Testament, served to guide him both personally and professionally. His stories, in fact, can be interpreted on multiple levels, much like the parables of the Bible.

Why the story of his faith is not more prominent in discussions of his life and work is a mystery to me. Is it because he had personal failings? Was he too harsh in his condemnation of hypocrisy in the church? Or would a frank discussion of his Christian faith make him less credible to secular audiences? Ultimately, it doesn't much matter. His novels will live on through the ages, revealing an author who cared deeply about mercy and justice, resisted evil in all its forms, and dared to believe that God is love. For those who have ears to hear, the "meaning" behind Charles Dickens's charming stories is as significant today as when he first wrote them.

THE WAY WAS FAMILIAR TO HIM—he traveled it frequently—but on this cold December morning in 1933, the old gentleman walked more tentatively than usual. Freezing temperatures overnight had created icy conditions on city streets and footpaths, and a heavy fog continued to linger over old London town. None of this dampened the old man's spirits, however. It was the Christmas season—his favorite time of year—a time to be joyful and thankful and kind!

As he made his way alongside the River Thames, the old gentleman's thoughts drifted back to the Christmases he had enjoyed so much as a child. His father, of course, had been the one to set the stage for festivities back then with a steady stream of friends who poured in and out of the big stone house on Gad's Hill. There was a never-ending stream of games to be played and charades for all ages and lively country dances that included the household servants as equal partners. In the evening, bright lights gave the exterior of the house a fairy-tale appearance, while laughter and music echoed down the hallways late into the night.

The old gentleman sighed involuntarily. How he longed for those bygone days!

"Good morning, Sir Harry, sir!"

The old gentleman looked up and raised his cane to acknowledge a passerby—a perfect stranger. Londoners often greeted him this way because of his famous father, but he, too, had his own claim to fame as a distinguished jurist and King's Counsel. "Sir Harry" they called him, an affectionate rendering of his birth name, Henry.

The fog was denser now. Sir Harry looked around to get his bearings and continued along the Thames Embankment. He wondered if it would snow this Christmas; it was certainly cold enough. He recalled with sudden emotion those numerous times when he and his brothers and sisters had gathered around their father in his study, a warm fire crackling nearby, to hear him read to them from a handwritten manuscript entitled *The Life of Our Lord*. It was a custom his father had observed every Christmas season. Even now, the opening lines reverberated in Sir Harry's memory.

My Dear Children,
I am very anxious that you should know something about the History of Jesus Christ. For everybody ought to know about Him. No one ever lived, who was so

good, so kind, so gentle, and so sorry for all people who did wrong, or were in any way ill or miserable, as He was. And as He is now in Heaven, where we hope to go, and all to meet each other after we are dead, and there be happy always together, you never can think what a good place Heaven is, without knowing who He was and what He did.[1]

It had now been more than sixty years since his father's passing. Each Christmas during the intervening decades, Sir Harry had kept family tradition alive by reading the very same manuscript to his own children (and now grandchildren). It was a deeply pleasurable experience that he looked forward to repeating in a fortnight or so.

Stepping off the Chelsea Embankment, Sir Harry raised his walking stick as a sign for oncoming traffic to yield and began to cross the road. He had no time to avoid the fast-approaching motorcycle, which had hit a patch of black ice and now hurtled toward him out of control. After being knocked unconscious to the icy ground and taken to a nearby hospital in Chelsea, Sir Harry clung precariously to life for the next two weeks, finally succumbing to his injuries a few days before Christmas. Sir Henry Fielding Dickens, the last surviving child of famed novelist Charles Dickens, lay dead at the age of eighty-four.

Thousands of Londoners mourned Sir Harry's death, but in a surprise twist that would have done justice to a scene from one of his father's novels, there was a final chapter of redemption. People had long assumed that Charles Dickens's last book was the unfinished novel *Edwin Drood*. But as events unfolded, the world learned of one remaining unpublished work—the very same handwritten manuscript Charles had read each year to his children at Christmastime, *The Life of Our Lord*. In essence, *The Life of Our Lord* was a harmony of the Gospels (peppered with Charles's personal asides and observations) intended for the private use and edification of the Dickens family, the children in particular. As such, Charles had never intended for it to be published.

In his will, however, Sir Henry left the following instructions regarding the manuscript:

> I give and bequeath to my wife the original manuscript of my father's "Life of Our Lord," which was bequeathed to my aunt Georgina Hogarth in my father's will, and given by her to me to hold on the following trusts:
>
> Being his son I have felt constrained to act upon my father's expressed desire that it should not be published, but I do not think it right that I should bind my children by any such view . . . I therefore direct that my wife and children should consider this question quite unfettered by any view of mine, and if by majority they decide . . . that it should be published, then I direct my wife to sell the same in trust and divide the net proceeds of such sale among my wife and all my children in equal shares.[2]

In February 1934, Lady Marie Fielding, Sir Henry's widow, sold *The Life of Our Lord* to the *Daily Mail* in London for $210,000. The *Daily Mail* in turn sold it to newspaper syndicates around the world. Hailed as "the literary find of a century," the Hearst newspaper chain in the United States released the story in weekly segments that so gripped the nation's reading public that pundits were led to proclaim that a national religious revival was at hand. Far from being the "dead horse" some newspaper publishers had initially considered the manuscript to be, *The Life of Our Lord* increased the circulation of every newspaper that carried it, while Simon & Schuster published a book version that became a nationwide bestseller.

Religious leaders were likewise effusive in their praise. "The time for the publication of *The Life of Our Lord* could not be more opportune," declared Samuel Cavert, general secretary of the Federal Churches of Christ.[3] His remarks were echoed by Dean Luther Weigle of the Yale Divinity School, who said, "Many people will read this because Charles Dickens wrote it and it will help to make many acquainted with the life of our Lord."[4]

All the hoopla leads one to wonder what Charles might have had to say. No doubt he would have appreciated the media attention, even if it was over a book he had never intended to publish. Throughout his career he had enjoyed the spotlight and now, nearly sixty-five years after his death, he was still making waves on both sides of the Atlantic.

He also would have been pleased—perhaps slightly chagrined—at the price the manuscript fetched, which was considerably more than he had received for any of his other books.

And what of the notion that the small volume he had written for the religious instruction of his children might serve as a catalyst in a worldwide spiritual awakening? What would he have thought of that? Even though such eminent writers as Fyodor Dostoyevsky and Leo Tolstoy referred to Charles Dickens as "that great Christian writer," he was not remembered as such in 1934. Nor was he thought of primarily in those terms while he lived. He often had harsh words for the church. Nor was he without scandal in his personal life. It was rumored that he left his wife, the mother of his ten children, for a much younger woman, an actress who became his mistress.

So where did Charles stand on questions of the Christian faith? Were the religious allusions in his writings a concession to the moral demands of his Victorian readership and not principles he shared personally? Might he have had some hidden motive for writing *The Life of Our Lord*, other than the obvious one of wanting to teach his children about Jesus Christ? His son, Sir Harry, seems to have put such questions to rest in *Memories of My Father*, a short book he wrote just a few years before his accidental death:

> His religious convictions, though he never made a parade of them, were very strong and deep, as appears by the letters he wrote to me and my brothers when we started our careers, as well as in the beautiful words of his will, which are most solemn and impressive in their religious devotion. So strong was this feeling, indeed, that he wrote the simple history of Our Lord's life for us when we were children.[5]

Whatever his faults may have been, Charles Dickens loved the Lord, and one would assume he would have been delighted to see millions of new readers, especially impressionable children, learning about Jesus the Savior. He knew all too well how elusive a happy childhood could be.

Born in Portsmouth, England, in 1812, Charles was the second child, and eldest son, of John and Elizabeth Dickens.

Around the time of his fifth birthday, the family moved to Chatham, Kent, where Charles enjoyed a somewhat idyllic life for the next six years. Not always in the best of health, and small for his age, Charles found welcome escape reading the popular romantic novels of his day and entertaining family and friends with imaginative plays and songs he had written. He also relished long walks in the surrounding countryside, often in the company of his father, with whom he enjoyed a good relationship. He was less close with his mother, but it was she who first taught him to read and write.

At the age of nine, Charles began his formal education at a nearby Christian school run by a young man named William Giles, the Oxford-educated son of a local Baptist minister. Undoubtedly, the Bible figured prominently in the school's curriculum, and throughout his life, Charles would hold Giles in the highest regard, crediting him for profoundly influencing his academic and moral development.

But dark days lay ahead.

Charles's father was not good at managing finances, and the family began to suffer, eventually relocating to the low-income neighborhood of Camden Town in London in 1822. Charles dropped out of school and was reduced to selling household property, including his precious books, at the nearby pawnshop. "I knew we got on very badly with the butcher and baker; that very often we had not too much for dinner; and that at last my father was arrested."[6]

As was the custom in those days, Elizabeth and the younger children joined John in his quarters at the debtors' prison in Marshalsea, while Charles and his older sister, Fanny, were left to fend for themselves. That was not much of a problem for Fanny since she was already a boarding student at a music academy. Twelve-year-old Charles, however, faced a bleak situation. He found lodgings with an impoverished elderly widow and faced an uncertain future, his dreams of becoming an educated and well-to-do gentleman irretrievably lost. "I know that, but for the mercy of God, I might easily have been, for any care that was taken of me, a little robber or a little vagabond."[7]

Through a family friend, Charles found a job at a rat-infested factory where he earned a paltry six shillings per week putting labels on pots of boot blacking. The hours were long and tedious, and the surroundings unhealthy, but what wore on Charles most was being separated from his family. It was a period of time during which he received "no advice, no counsel, no encouragement, no consolation, no support from anyone that I can call to mind, so help me God."[8]

When a relative died and left a bequest to the Dickens family, Charles's father was able to pay off his debts and leave prison with his brood. In time, Charles managed to begin his education again, but he was forever changed by the experience of living on his own, his "whole nature . . . penetrated with grief and humiliation." Nonetheless, those hard times served as the animus for many of his novels and inspired the social activism for which he likewise became famous.

Charles's literary success began early in life and stemmed from his work as a court reporter and political journalist. He was an exceptionally keen observer of human nature and had a wonderful way of capturing the everyday nuances of common folk. He first began writing stories as weekly and monthly installments in journals—stories that were later reprinted in book form.

Success came quickly.

The Pickwick Papers was followed by *Oliver Twist*, *Nicholas Nickleby*, *The Old Curiosity Shop*, *Barnaby Rudge*, and in 1843, when he was but thirty-one years old, *A Christmas Carol*.

In 1846, he started *The Life of Our Lord*, finishing it in 1849. Also in 1849, he began writing *David Copperfield* (the most autobiographical of his novels), followed by *Hard Times*, *Little Dorrit*, *A Tale of Two Cities*, and in 1861, *Great Expectations*.

Never fully at ease with his international acclaim and ever-increasing wealth, Charles pushed himself unrelentingly to do more. He traveled widely, making two trips to the United States where he gave well-attended public readings of his works. He also became heavily involved in charitable works, including fighting for prison reform, improving childhood education, and running a shelter for prostitutes.

Charles decried what he saw as the unresponsiveness of the established church to the pressing social needs of his day, flirting for a time with the notion of becoming a Unitarian. But he never forsook the Anglican Church and remained a lay Anglican all his life.

Responding by letter in 1861 to criticism from a churchman that his books lacked a portrayal of strong Christian characters, he wrote:

All my strongest illustrations are derived from the New Testament; all my social abuses are shown as departures from its spirit; all my good people are humble, charitable, faithful and forgiving. Over and over again, I claim them in express words as disciples of the Founder of our religion; but I must admit that to a man (or woman) they all arise and wash their faces, and do not appear unto men to fast.[9]

The latter reference to fasting from Jesus's Sermon on the Mount well describes the quiet but ardent faith to which Charles subscribed in his personal life, and which he also drew upon as a writer to craft his unforgettable stories.

On June 9, 1865, Charles was aboard the train involved in the Staplehurst rail crash in Britain that claimed ten lives. At the time he had been working on *Our Mutual Friend*, which like his other books was being released in serial format. He was never quite the same after the accident. He lost his voice for two weeks following the wreck and was anxious when traveling anywhere by train. His literary output declined but not his demanding schedule of public readings, his social service, or his dedication to his family.

In September 1868, he bade a tearful farewell to his youngest son, Edward Bulwer Lytton, nicknamed Plorn, who was traveling to Australia to attend university. Over the following months, Charles could not stop thinking about Plorn and his welfare, and on Christmas Day wrote him a letter, saying in part,

> I put a New Testament among your books for the very same reasons and with the very same hopes that made me write an easy account of it for you when you were a little child; because it is the best book that ever was or will be known in the world, and because it teaches you the best lessons by which any human creature who tries to be truthful and faithful to duty can possibly be guided. As your brothers have gone away, one by one, I have written to each such words as I am now writing you, and have entreated them all to guide themselves by this book, putting aside the interpretations and inventions of men . . . I most solemnly impress upon you the truth and beauty of the Christian religion, as it came

from Christ Himself, and the impossibility of you going far wrong if you humbly but heartily respect it.[10]

Charles continued his hectic pace, starting a new book, *Edwin Drood*, even as his health worsened. On June 8, 1870, after taking a long walk through the beautiful countryside around Gad's Hill, he suffered a stroke and died the following day at fifty-eight years old. A printed epitaph that was circulated at the time of his death read, "He was a sympathiser with the poor, the suffering, and the oppressed; and by his death, one of England's greatest writers is lost to the world."[11]

Perhaps the best testament as to who Charles Dickens really was, insofar as his Christian faith is concerned, is contained in his own words as they appear in his last will and testament:

> I direct that my name be inscribed in plain English letters on my tomb, without the addition of "Mr." or "Esquire." I conjure my friends on no account to make me the subject of any monument, memorial, or testimonial whatever. I rest my claims to the remembrance of my country upon my published works, and to the remembrance of my friends upon their experience of me in addition thereto. I commit my soul to the mercy of God through our Lord and Saviour Jesus Christ, and I exhort my dear children humbly to try to guide themselves by the teaching of the New Testament in its broad spirit, and to put no faith in any man's narrow construction of its letter here or there. In witness whereof I the said Charles Dickens, the testator, have to this my last Will and Testament set my hand this 12th day of May in the year of our Lord 1869.[12]

As a writer and filmmaker, I'm inspired by the life of Charles Dickens. He knew the rock from whence he had been hewn and made it his chief aim to educate not only his children but also all people in "the teachings of our great Master and unostentatiously to lead the reader up to those teachings as the great source of all moral goodness."[13]

In whatever way I can, I hope to be among those who continue his legacy.

John D. Rockefeller Sr.

Have you ever been to Lyford Cay in the Bahamas? Chances are you have not. And chances are I never would have been, either, had my sister not married a shipping magnate who owned a house there. Located on the western tip of New Providence Island, Lyford Cay is one of the world's most exclusive neighborhoods. It's a millionaire's playground where everything is discreetly private—from the championship golf course to the tennis club and yachting marina to the private international school to the mile-long beach.

I visited twice during my twenties along with other members of the family, and we all stayed at my sister's house, each in our own bedroom. My brothers enjoyed playing tennis, but I preferred the water, spending many delightful hours swimming and snorkeling off the white sand beach.

I also took several walks with my father, which I treasured. You need to understand that the best communication with my father typically took place in the context of a walk. He was not a talkative man by nature, but there was something about walking that seemed to loosen his tongue and draw our spirits closer together.

Late one afternoon, as we walked past the sumptuous villas in the neighborhood where my sister lived, I commented, "These people sure have a lot of money. How does anyone get to be so rich?"

Dad kicked at a scraggly weed that had somehow managed to gain a foothold on the pristine sidewalk. "They earn as much as they can, and they can as much as they can, and then they sit on top of the can," said Dad in a singsong voice.

"They're tightwads, you mean."

"Well, a lot of them probably are. But one thing's for sure. You don't get rich by giving away your money." I nodded, and we continued our walk. If I had known better, I might have asked my dad if he'd heard the story of John D. Rockefeller Sr. I don't mean the story of his children or grandchildren but of the man who started the family fortune—the first billionaire and possibly the richest person who has ever lived.

HE CUT A FINE FIGURE AT SIX FEET TALL with broad shoulders and wide-set blue eyes, a square jaw and handsome face, always nattily dressed with small diamonds sparkling on his vest and a wad of cash in his trousers. Such was the physical appearance of William Avery ("Big Bill") Rockefeller.

Big Bill, who was in the habit of leaving home for months at a time, would typically reappear out of the blue behind a team of fine horses, thrilling his children with tales of his adventures—meeting Iroquois chieftains and famous personalities of the day, traveling on great paddlewheel steamboats, visiting the big cities, and winning shooting competitions. For several weeks, sometimes months, all would be well at home. The Rockefellers were a family again. And then, as abruptly as he had appeared, Big Bill would take off again to who knows where.

Admittedly, he possessed a number of virtues in addition to his erstwhile charms. He didn't smoke or drink, and he made it a point to promptly settle his tab at the local store and pay off the bills his family had incurred during his absence. He was entrepreneurial—he ran a logging business and sawmill for a time—and believed in the sanctity of contracts. He enjoyed music and laughter, and his wife and children surely loved him. They just had a hard time understanding him, as did most of the townsfolk in the succession of villages in upstate New York where the Rockefeller family lived.

After all, just what did Big Bill do for a living?

No one could quite figure it out.

Then one day Big Bill was spotted in a neighboring town posing as a doctor selling elixirs—so-called "botanical cures" guaranteed to heal cancer (except in the most advanced cases, and even then they were able to do at least *some* good). From that day on, Big Bill was known among the locals—often with a knowing smile—as "Doc" Rockefeller.

As his family grew and his absences from home became increasingly lengthy, it fell to Doc's wife, Eliza Davison Rockefeller, to raise the children on her own. By all accounts, she did an outstanding job. She was a plain-looking, plainspoken woman of Puritan roots, a strict disciplinarian, and deeply religious. Her education was limited, but she knew her Bible well. She had a calm temperament and taught her children to economize and work hard.

Her oldest son, John Davison Rockefeller, was born on July 8, 1839, in the town of Richford, New York, halfway between Ithaca and Binghamton. He took after his mother in most respects. He was solemn and even-tempered, mature beyond his years. His brothers and sisters knew him to have a droll sense of humor and a sensitive, caring nature, but he tended to guard his deeper feelings and emotions from strangers. He was slow and deliberate when making decisions, weighing every possible option and then acting decisively when his mind was set. Eliza leaned on him heavily when her husband wasn't around, which was most of the time, and the boy-man came to realize early on that his family largely depended on him to fill his father's shoes.

The first wage John D. earned was $1.50 for a week's worth of work performed for neighbors. Dutifully, he turned the money over to his mother. The small sum could easily have disappeared into the sea of Rockefeller family need, but Eliza used the moment to teach John D. a lesson. She told him it would please her greatly if he would pay a tithe on his income, which John gladly did that Sunday when he put fifteen cents into the offering plate at church. This simple act marked the beginning of a spiritual discipline that would stay with him the rest of his life. "I was trained from the beginning to work and to save," he said in later years. "I have always regarded it as a religious duty to get all I could honorably and to give all I could."[1]

He learned another valuable lesson several years later when he loaned fifty dollars to a neighboring farmer at 7 percent interest. A year passed, and the farmer paid back the loan plus $3.50 in interest. It was a revelation for John. He had been hoeing potatoes at the time, receiving thirty-seven and a half cents a day for his work (a decent wage at the time for a twelve-year-old). But the $3.50 he now held in his hand was something altogether different. It was the equivalent of ten days' work, only there had been no work. At least, not on his part. Rather, the money he had loaned out had gone to work for him. As he would reminisce, "The impression was gaining ground with me that it was a good thing to let the money be my slave and not make myself a slave to the money."[2]

It was an impression grounded in Scripture—"Thou shalt lend unto many nations, but thou shalt not borrow; and thou shalt reign over many nations, but they shall not reign over thee" (Deut. 15:6)—and strengthened by his mother's homilies and prayers. "Willful waste makes woeful want," she was fond of saying to her children.[3]

Eliza impressed other Christian graces on her youngsters as well, including the need to extend forgiveness and seek reconciliation. When the children went to bed at night, they turned to one another and asked forgiveness for anything they may have done or said during the day to cause harm or hurt.

Big Bill, meanwhile, was up to old tricks and was now a suspected horse thief. He was too cagey to get caught in the act, but others in his gang were arrested and sent to prison.

There was also the matter of Big Bill's perpetually roving eye. He had been in the custom of hiring a housekeeper to help with his wife's household needs. And, apparently, to help with some of his own. John D., in fact, had two half-sisters from his father's liaisons with one such domestic, Nancy Brown.

In 1849, Big Bill became embroiled in fresh scandal that earned him a new nickname—"Devil Bill." In papers filed at nearby Auburn Courthouse, he was accused of having raped Anne Vanderbeak the year before. Anne, a tall and comely lass from Moravia, New York, had been hired as household help for Eliza. Devil Bill never stood trial in the case and spent the next several months on the move, eventually relocating his family to Owego near the Pennsylvania state line. (One assumes he wanted access to a quick getaway should it become necessary.)

Eliza seems to have reconciled herself to a long and desultory marriage to her rake of a husband, while John D. worked hard to distinguish himself in his new school, Owego Academy. He was an average student, not exceptional, though he did show an aptitude for numbers.

Three years passed, and just when it appeared the Rockefeller children were gaining a sense of order and stability in Owego, their peripatetic father pulled up stakes again and moved the household to the small town of Strongsville, Ohio, twelve miles outside Cleveland. In Owego the Rockefellers had lived in their own house, but in Strongsville they were obliged to share cramped quarters with Devil Bill's sister and brother-in-law and their children.

In the fall of 1853, after an absence of many months plying his "trade," Devil Bill resurfaced in Strongsville to check on his family. After deciding that John and William needed more exposure to the wider world, he placed them in a boardinghouse in downtown Cleveland and enrolled them in school. Their landlady, Mrs. Woodin, took a maternal interest in the brothers and introduced them to her church nearby, the Erie Street Baptist Church.

True to form, John D. maintained a steady course in his new surroundings. He began studying at Central High School and also became a regular at Mrs. Woodin's church, where he grew particularly close to one of the deacons, an older man named Alexander Sked. John D., who had received religious instruction at his mother's knee and had dutifully attended church throughout his childhood, found something new and exciting about Deacon Sked's brand of faith. A native of Scotland, the deacon was not ashamed to express his faith in an overt and demonstrative way, raising his hands in the sanctuary and praying and singing in a loud and impassioned voice. He was genuinely kind as well as godly, and the brothers saw in him a father figure they would do well to emulate.

John D. became increasingly open to the gospel message, and it wasn't long before he responded to an invitation to make Christ his Lord and Savior. In the fall of 1854, Deacon Sked baptized him in the church baptistery.

Meanwhile, quite a contrasting tale was unfolding in the life of Devil Bill. A pretty young woman across the border in Canada had caught his eye, and he had courted her in his dashing and winsome way. Posing as Dr. Levingston (he appears to have contrived the name from Livingston, New York, the birthplace of his father), Devil Bill married the unsuspecting Margaret Allen at a ceremony in Nichols, New York, on June 12, 1855.

A month before this bigamous marriage took place, the good doctor had entreated John D. to drop out of high school and enroll in a three-month program of study at E. G. Folsom's Business College. In retrospect, it seems Bill was grooming his oldest and most responsible son to be the father he was not. And though he would continue to pop in and out of John D.'s life for the next half-century until his death at the ripe old age of ninety-six, Devil Bill became a more and more distant figure in his first family's life.

Unaware of any ulterior motive on his father's part, John D. conceded the wisdom of preparing sooner rather than later for a career in business and dropped out of high school to learn double-entry bookkeeping and business management at Folsom's. His decision came as a shock to Eliza, who had cherished hopes of her son going to college and becoming a Baptist minister.

After graduating from Folsom's that August, John D. began a long and difficult search for employment, finally succeeding on September 26, 1855, when the mercantile firm of Hewitt and Tuttle in downtown Cleveland hired him as an assistant bookkeeper. From then on, September 26 became "Job Day" on John D.'s calendar, which he celebrated with as much gusto and fanfare as any of his many birthdays.

He started the workday punctually at 6:30 a.m., having brought a box lunch with him, and stayed well into the night, poring over the company's books. Among his duties were reviewing invoices and expenditures down to the penny, drafting contracts, and collecting money from various rental properties. He was a stickler for detail and impressed his employers early on with his thoroughness and unwavering honesty. For three months he labored without pay—not unusual during that time, when new employees were put through an apprenticeship, or trial period. On January 2, 1856, Isaac Hewitt gave John D. fifty dollars in back pay and offered him full-time employment at a salary of twenty-five dollars per month. John D. was ecstatic but cautious. He prayed for God to protect him from pride and greed.

Tellingly, the same scrupulous approach John D. applied at Hewitt and Tuttle governed his own finances. Before he received a dime of salary, he purchased a small red book, which he called "Ledger A," and in it he recorded all of his personal transactions down to the penny. The first entry in Ledger A recorded a gift of ten cents to "the Missionary Cause." Other annotations followed in quick order: a gift of ten cents to Mr. Downe, the young minister at Erie Street Baptist Church, one dollar for his pew rental, various donations to missionaries and church workers, a gift of twenty-five cents to his beloved Deacon Sked.

This pattern of working hard and giving generously would define the course of John D.'s long life. Though he came under intense scrutiny in later years for the business practices he employed to become the world's first billionaire, Ledger A is early proof that he was a generous person.

There was a reason for his generosity, as John D. never hesitated to say. "God gave me my money," he said simply in later years. "I believe the power to make money is a gift from God—just as are the instincts for art, music, literature, the doctor's talent, the nurse's . . . Having been endowed with the gift I possess, I believe it is my duty to make money and still more money, and to use the money I make for the good of my fellow man according to the dictates of my conscience."[4] Again, John D. was on solid scriptural footing: "Thou shalt remember the Lord thy God: for it is he that giveth thee power to get wealth, that he may establish his covenant which he sware unto thy fathers, as it is this day" (Deut. 8:18).

On April 1, 1858, not yet nineteen years old, John D. dedicated a new business to the Lord—Clark and Rockefeller. He and his partner, Maurice Clark, whom he had met at Folsom's Business College, were their own bosses in a produce commission house. The business prospered, and John D.'s charitable giving increased. The recipients were much the same as before—churches and missionaries, the poor and homeless, an orphanage. Other gifts revealed his views on the social issues of the day. Convinced of the justice of abolition, he gave a man in Cincinnati the necessary money to buy his wife out of slavery. And throughout, he maintained a growing involvement in his own local church, looking after Erie Street Baptist as though it were his own home.

He lovingly swept and mopped the church floors, washed the windows, replaced the burned-out candles along the walls, and stoked the furnace with wood in wintertime. On Sunday mornings, he would ring the church bell, calling the faithful to prayer. He regularly attended Friday evening prayer meetings, taught a Bible study each Wednesday night, and was a regular at both worship services on Sunday. When the church was on the verge of closing its doors due to foreclosure on its mortgage, John D. spearheaded a drive to raise the money necessary to pay off the debt. The thankful church leadership appointed him a trustee.

When he wasn't at church, John D. was at work. He was the first to arrive in the morning and the last to leave at night, usually hunched over the tall bookkeeper's table, scrutinizing the company's ledger books under the light of a whale-oil lamp. He did not attend dances or parties and never frequented the theater.

After the outbreak of the Civil War, John D. considered enlisting in the army. But given the unreliability of his father (who he had by now discovered was a bigamist), John D. considered it more important to provide financially for his mother and other family members. So he did what many young men of means did at the time—he paid for a substitute soldier to take his place and continued working.

The Civil War years saw his business partnership expand and prosper, and in 1864 he married Laura "Cettie" Spelman, whom he had first met at Central High when he was fifteen. (Cettie had been valedictorian of her senior class.) Like John D.'s mother, Cettie came from Puritan forbears, her parents having moved to Ohio from Massachusetts before she was born. When John D. began calling on her, she worked as a teacher and assistant principal at the Hudson Street School, enjoying her work immensely, content to remain where she was until something better came along. That "something better" proved to be married life with the tall, somewhat stoop-shouldered, and intensely focused John D. Rockefeller.

By all accounts their marriage was a happy one, and they produced five children together. (One, Alice, lived but thirteen months.) Cettie, like her husband, was a devout Christian and created a beautiful and stable home life that served as a haven for the hardworking John D. "Oh! For a home dinner, good cream and the quiet and peace of our table," he once wrote her in a letter while away on business.[5]

The pattern of his life was now set—God, family, work. All that remained was for John D. to become rich. And rich he became. Without question he possessed the necessary qualities to become successful at most any business, but it was the oil business that ultimately made John D.'s fortune.

In 1863, as a side venture, John D. and Maurice Clark (now joined in their partnership by Maurice's two brothers and an English-born chemist named Samuel Andrews) constructed an oil refinery in Cleveland to take advantage of the oil drilling frenzy sweeping the nation. At the time kerosene, extracted from petroleum, had largely replaced whale oil as an illuminant, so the market potential was clear. But it was a turbulent, highly speculative time in the nascent petroleum business. Fortunes were being made—and frequently lost—overnight.

After carefully weighing the pros and cons, John D. decided to stake his fortune on oil as the growth commodity of the future. For two years he scrimped and saved and in February 1865 bought out his partners (Samuel Andrews stayed on), taking over the company that would become Standard Oil of Ohio and eventually make him the richest person in the world.

Criticized by some for his monopolistic methods, John D. transformed a chaotic and cutthroat business into one of order and efficiency that would vastly benefit the American people. He introduced cost-saving measures to every aspect of the refining business, creating superior products at lower prices than ever before. The price of kerosene, for instance, dropped from twenty-three to seven cents a gallon. And the Standard Oil brand was of finer quality by far than any other! Furthermore, at a time when most oil-refining companies were heedlessly polluting the environment by dumping their waste in the closest lake or river, Standard Oil was inventing ways of creating every kind of by-product imaginable from the "black gold"—from gasoline to power their plant machinery (the automobile was not yet in commercial production) to synthetic beeswax, eye makeup, and Vaseline.

By 1879, John D. and Standard Oil controlled 90 percent of the world's oil refining operations. Within a few years they had taken over 90 percent of the oil distribution market and a third of all the operational oil wells in the world.

There were those who begrudged the mogul his success and accused him of strong-arm tactics in absorbing his competitors, but his own conscience was clear. It was no sin to be better organized, harder working, and more efficient than one's business rivals. His was not the only fortune being made during the so-called Gilded Age of American industry. Andrew Carnegie, J. P. Morgan, and Cornelius Vanderbilt are a few of the names that come to mind. But the ever-growing fortune of John D. Rockefeller was certainly the most honestly gained.

And the giving continued. "It seemed as if I was favored and got increase because the Lord knew I was going to turn around and give it back."[6]

As his fame and generosity spread, John D. began receiving hundreds—later tens of thousands—of letters each month from people around the world asking for financial help. In the beginning he considered each request on its merits, but before long the demand was simply too overwhelming, even with a large staff sorting through the trunkloads of mail.

To help him forge a new paradigm for his charitable giving, John D. hired Reverend Frederick Gates, a Baptist minister and secretary of the American Baptist Education Society. The two had met in 1888 when Reverend Gates approached John D. for start-up funds for a major Baptist university in the Midwest. John D. liked what he heard and over time contributed $80 million (more than $2 billion in today's currency) to what became the University of Chicago.

By all accounts, Reverend Gates was an innovative thinker with a brilliant mind for business. Under John D.'s employ, he took a scientific approach to philanthropy, addressing not so much the symptoms of problems as the underlying causes, which, if properly addressed, could result in positive and lasting change. John D., with the guidance of Reverend Gates, became a major benefactor of medical science and improvements in education throughout the country.

By 1902, John D. had amassed a $200 million fortune, an astonishing figure considering that the gross domestic product (GDP) of the United States at the time was $20 billion. Only a few people were aware that he had actually retired from the day-to-day management of Standard Oil and had dedicated himself to giving his fortune away. John D.'s son, John David Rockefeller, known as Junior, who had been mentored under Reverend Gates, stepped into his own in 1913 as president of the Rockefeller Foundation, which was launched with an initial endowment of $100 million "to promote the well-being of mankind throughout the world."

Thanks to John D.'s philanthropy, numerous schools, churches, and hospitals were built around the world. Missionaries were sent abroad, while privately funded teams of scientists discovered cures for yellow fever, meningitis, and hookworm. John D. gave tens of millions of dollars to higher education, including historically black universities and Baptist colleges.

Satisfied that his assets were being well handled, John D. made time in the latter part of his life for what mattered most—spending time with his family and his God. And playing golf, of course! He and Cettie celebrated their golden wedding anniversary on September 8, 1914, prompting John D.

to declare, "I have had but one sweetheart, and I am thankful to say that I still have her."[7]

As a boy, John D. had famously stated he wanted to grow up to be worth $100,000 and live to be a hundred years old. Uncharacteristically, he erred by a wide margin on the financial side, but did come reasonably close on his projected lifespan. After his beloved Cettie died in 1915, he lived another twenty-two years, enjoying life to the fullest. He faithfully attended church, taught Sunday school, played golf, and got a big kick out of giving away shiny new dimes to children and perfect strangers, exhorting them always to be good stewards of God's manifold gifts.

When John D. died peacefully in his sleep on May 23, 1937, his assets (to large degree safeguarded through the foundations he had started) equaled 1.5 percent of America's GDP. In modern terms, his net worth exceeded $350 billion. And that was just half of John D.'s fortune.

The other half he had given away.

Dad had come to visit me in Belize. He was ninety-one years old. We took a walk near the Cahal Pech Pyramids in San Ignacio Town near where I was living at the time. His heart had been giving him trouble, so we walked slowly. I held his arm most of the way, and we just took our time.

We enjoyed a nice Belizean lunch later at the local hotel when Dad took out his wallet and showed us his "business" card. It identified him as chairman of the Stewards Foundation, a nonprofit organization dedicated to teaching the sport of rowing (crew) to young people. With a glow of pride in his eyes, he told my wife, Cheryl, and me of all the good the foundation had been doing in the Tampa community, helping youngsters from lower-income families improve their chances for college, and giving disabled veterans, many of them using prosthetic limbs, the opportunity to re-engage in team sport and improve their mental health.

My dad had been a success in many areas of life—first in the field of commercial aviation and later as a businessman. The Stewards Foundation was something relatively new for him, and he received no salary for his efforts. Yet here he was, in the twilight of life, talking mostly about the satisfaction he had received from giving to others.

Two months later I found myself in Tampa, sitting by my father's bed, holding his hand as he lay dying. His mind was clear. During the last five or so years of his life he had turned to the Lord under the preaching of a Presbyterian minister in town. I think he had also been touched by the friendships he had formed at church. He was ready to meet the Lord. Near the end Dad looked at me and said, "All things come to an end. I'm not sad or unhappy. I've left my mark. My family is my mark."

When I take a walk again one day with my father, I'd like to think we'll pass by many mansions as we did that day in Lyford Cay in the Bahamas all those years ago. But the mansions on this walk will far eclipse anything we saw then. For they will not be built with human hands. And they will not be for sale at any price.

And in that place I don't know that John D. Rockefeller Sr. will have the greatest and most splendid mansion of the lot. His may be among the smaller ones for all I know. The greatest mansions, in fact, may belong to the least among us—those who the world never knew. "For man looks at the outward appearance, but the LORD looks at the heart" (1 Sam. 16:7 NASB). What I do know—what I firmly believe—is that John D., like many who have come before and many who will follow after, will one day hear his Master's voice saying, "Well done, thou good and faithful servant: thou hast been faithful over a few things, I will make thee ruler over many things: enter thou into the joy of thy lord" (Matt. 25:21, 23).

NOTES

Dag Hammarskjöld

1. Dag Hammarskjöld, *Markings*, trans. Leif Sjöberg and W. H. Auden (New York: Alfred A. Knopf, 1964), i.
2. Roger Lipsey, *Hammarskjöld: A Life* (Ann Arbor, MI: University of Michigan Press, 2013), 118.
3. Hammarskjöld, *Markings*, 89.
4. Ibid., 90.
5. Ibid., 91.
6. "Dag Hammarskjöld," United Nations Dag Hammarskjöld Library, accessed October 8, 2015, research.un.org/c.php?g=98287&p=924330.
7. Ibid.
8. United Nations, General Assembly Seventh Session, Official Records, Friday, April 10, 1953.
9. Wilder Foote, ed., *Servant of Peace: A Selection of the Speeches and Statements of Dag Hammarskjöld, Secretary-General of the United Nations, 1953–1961* (New York: Harper and Row, 1962), 23.
10. Peter B. Heller, *The United Nations under Dag Hammarskjöld, 1953–1961* (Lanham, MD: Scarecrow Press, 2001), 40.
11. Ibid., 41.
12. Hammarskjöld, *Markings*, 100.
13. Ibid., 142.
14. Ibid., 143.
15. Ibid., 156.
16. Ibid., 159, 166.
17. "World: A Royal Funeral," *Time*, October 6, 1961.

18. Arthur L. Gavshon, *The Mysterious Death of Dag Hammarskjöld* (New York: Walker and Company, 1962), 178.
19. Hammarskjöld, *Markings*, 122.

Frederick Douglass

1. This story is based on Douglass's three autobiographies, *Narrative of the Life of Frederick Douglass, an American Slave* (1845), *My Bondage and My Freedom* (1855), and *Life and Times of Frederick Douglass* (1881, 1892).

Florence Nightingale

1. Mark Bostridge, *Florence Nightingale: The Making of an Icon* (New York: Farrar, Straus and Giroux, 2008), 50.
2. Ibid., 50.
3. Cecil Woodham-Smith, *Florence Nightingale* (New York: McGraw-Hill, 1951), 9.
4. Bostridge, *The Making of an Icon*, 54.
5. Florence Nightingale, *Florence Nightingale: An Introduction to Her Life and Family*, vol. 1 of *Collected Works of Florence Nightingale*, ed. Lynn McDonald (Waterloo, Ontario: Wilfrid Laurier University Press, 2001), 286.
6. Bostridge, *The Making of an Icon*, 54.
7. Woodham-Smith, *Florence Nightingale*, 22.
8. Sir Edward Tyas Cook, *The Life of Florence Nightingale*, vol. 1 (London: Macmillan, 1913), 60.
9. Woodham-Smith, *Florence Nightingale*, 35.
10. Ibid., 49.
11. Nightingale, *Florence Nightingale's Spiritual Journey*, vol. 2, 373.
12. Woodham-Smith, *Florence Nightingale*, 35.
13. Richard Stone, *Some British Empiricists in the Social Sciences, 1650–1900* (Cambridge: Cambridge University Press, 1997), 311.
14. Woodham-Smith, *Florence Nightingale*, 85.

Frank País

1. José Alvarez, *Frank País: Architect of Cuba's Betrayed Revolution* (Boca Raton, FL: Universal-Publishers, 2009), 65.
2. W. John Green, *A History of Political Murder in Latin America: Killing the Messengers of Change* (Albany: State University of New York Press, 2015), 91–92.
3. Juan Antonio Monroy, *Frank País: Líder evangélico en la Revolución Cubana* (Terrassa, España: Editorial CLIE, 2003), 82.

Fyodor Dostoyevsky

1. Carole Bos, "Dostoevsky," Awesome Stories, published July 1, 2006, http://www.awesomestories.com/asset/view/Dostoevsky.

2. Orest Miller and Nikolay Strakhov, *Biografiya, pis'ma i zametki iz zapis-noi knizhki F.M. Dostoevskogo* (St. Petersburg, 1863), 119, as quoted in Joseph Frank, *Dostoyevsky: A Writer in His Time* (Princeton: Princeton University Press, 2009), 178.

3. Ibid., 181–82.

4. Ibid., 183.

5. Fyodor Dostoyevsky, *A Writer's Diary*, quoted by Joseph Frank in *Dostoyevsky: The Years of Ordeal, 1850–1859* (Princeton: Princeton University Press, 1986), 73.

6. Ibid., 188–89.

7. Fyodor Dostoevsky, *House of the Dead* (St. Petersburg, 1862), quoted in Frank, *A Writer in His Time*, 199.

8. Ibid., 201.

9. F. M. Dostoevsky, *Pis'ma*, vol. 1 (Moscow, 1928–1959), 142, quoted in Frank, *A Writer in His Time*, 220.

10. Feodor Dostoyevsky, *The House of the Dead or Prison Life in Siberia* (New York: E. P. Dutton & Co., 1911), 368.

11. Fyodor Dostoyevsky, *Selected Letters of Fyodor Dostoyevsky*, ed. Joseph Frank and David I. Goldstein, trans. Andrew R. MacAndrew (New Brunswick, NJ: Rutgers University Press, 1987), 469–70.

12. Anna Dostoevsky, *Reminiscences*, trans. and ed. Beatrice Stillman (New York: Liveright Publishing, 1975), 345–46.

13. F. W. Boreham, *The Prodigal: Sidelights on an Immortal Story* (London: The Epworth Press, 1941), 88–89.

14. Fyodor Dostoyevsky, *An Honest Thief and Other Stories* (Rockville, MD: Wildside Press, 2008), 246.

Jean-Henri Dunant

1. Jean-Henri Dunant, *A Memory of Solferino* (Washington, DC: American National Red Cross, 1959), 41.

2. Ibid., 44, 50.

3. YMCA Europe, *The Paris Basis of 1855*, accessed July 27, 2015, http://www.ymcaeurope.com/data/files/paris-basis-34.pdf.

4. Dunant, *A Memory of Solferino*, 115–16.

5. "Who Was the Father of the Red Cross?" Swiss Info, May 8, 2009, http://www.swissinfo.ch/eng/who-was-the-father-of-the-red-cross-/3666.

6. John G. Simmons, *Doctors and Discoveries: Lives That Created Today's Medicine* (Boston: Houghton Mifflin, 2002), 409.

7. Caroline Moorehead, *Dunant's Dream: War, Switzerland and the History of the Red Cross* (New York: Carroll & Graf Publishers, 1998), 18.

Abraham Lincoln

1. Charles Carleton Coffin, *Abraham Lincoln* (New York: Harper & Brothers, 1892), 28.

2. G. Frederick Owen, *Abraham Lincoln: The Man & His Faith* (Carol Stream, IL: Tyndale, 1981), 5.

3. Ibid., 10.

4. John Wesley Hill, *Abraham Lincoln: Man of God* (New York: Putnam's Sons, 1920), 321–22.

5. William J. Johnson, *Abraham Lincoln: The Christian* (New York: Eaton & Mains, 1913), 50.

6. Author's paraphrase combining truths from Romans 9:19; Psalm 102:11; and Ecclesiastes 1:14.

7. Johnson, *Abraham Lincoln*, 52–53.

8. Mary Lincoln to James Smith, June 8, 1870, in Justin G. Turner and Linda Levitt Turner, *Mary Todd Lincoln: Her Life and Letters* (New York: Fromm International Publishing Corp., 1987), 567.

9. Johnson, *Abraham Lincoln*, 58.

10. Don E. Fehrenbacher and Virginia Fehrenbacher, eds., *Recollected Words of Abraham Lincoln* (Stanford, CA: Stanford University Press, 1996), 374.

11. Bruce Chadwick, *Lincoln for President: An Unlikely Candidate, an Audacious Strategy, and the Victory No One Saw Coming* (Naperville, IL: Sourcebooks, 2010), 308.

12. Hill, *Man of God*, 169–70.

13. Abraham Lincoln, *Collected Works of Abraham Lincoln*, vol. 4, ed. Roy P. Basier (New Brunswick, NJ: Rutgers University Press, 1953), 271.

14. Hill, *Man of God*, 283.

15. Paul M. Angle, ed., *The Lincoln Reader* (Westport, CT: Greenwood Press, 1947), 428–30.

16. Carl Sandburg, *Abraham Lincoln: The War Years* (New York: Harcourt, Brace, 1939), 379–80.

17. Fehrenbacher and Fehrenbacher, *Recollected Words*, 388.

18. Abraham Lincoln, *The Complete Works of Abraham Lincoln*, vol. 4, ed. John G. Nicolay and John Hay (New York: Tandy Company, 1905), 209–10.

19. Shelby Foote, *The Civil War,* vol. 3 (New York: Random House, 1974), 903.

20. Owen, *The Man and His Faith*, 205.

21. Stephen Mansfield, *Lincoln's Battle with God: A President's Struggle with Faith and What It Meant for America* (Nashville: Thomas Nelson, 2012), xvii.

22. "President Abraham Lincoln Assassinated," Civil War Trust, accessed August 27, 2015, http://www.civilwar.org/education/history/end-of-war/lincoln-assassinated.html?referrer=https://www.google.com/.

Joseph Lister and Louis Pasteur

1. James Joseph Walsh, *Makers of Modern Medicine* (New York: Fordham University Press, 1915), 318.

2. Laurence Farmer, *Master Surgeon: A Biography of Joseph Lister* (New York: Harper & Row, 1962), 28–29.

3. René Jules Dubos, *Louis Pasteur, Free Lance of Science* (New York: Scribner, 1960), 85.

4. Iris Noble, *The Courage of Dr. Lister* (New York: Julian Messner, 1960), 57.

5. G.T. Wrench, MD, *Lord Lister: His Life and Work* (London: Unwin Brothers, 1913), 12.

6. René Vallery-Radot, *The Life of Pasteur* (New York: McClure, Phillips & Co., 1902), 157.

7. Paul De Kruif, *Microbe Hunters* (New York: Harcourt, Brace, 1926), 59.

8. Michael Patrick Leahy, *Letter to an Atheist* (Thompsons Station, TN: Harpeth River Press, 2007), 61.

9. Vallery-Radot, *The Life of Pasteur*, 463.

10. Ibid., 462.

11. Ibid., 464.

12. Sir Rickman John Godlee, *Lord Lister* (London: Macmillan, 1918), 613.

13. Ibid., 552.

14. E. Salaman, "A Talk with Einstein," *The Listener* 54 (1955): 370–71, quoted in Max Jammer, *Einstein and Religion: Physics and Theology* (Princeton: Princeton University Press, 1999), 123.

15. Hector Charles Cameron, *Joseph Lister, the Friend of Man* (London: W. Heinemann Publishers, 1948), 67.

Chiune Sugihara

1. Christian Leitz, *Nazi Foreign Policy, 1933–1941: The Road to Global War* (London: Routledge, 2004), 126.

2. Mordecai Paldiel, *Diplomat Heroes of the Holocaust* (Jersey City, NJ: KTAV Publishing House, 2007), 51.

3. Ibid., 52.

4. Christine Faye Kohler, *Leaflets of Our Resistance*, vol. 2 (Los Angeles: Exclamation! Publishers, 2011), 37.

5. Ibid.

6. Ibid.

7. Hillel Levine, *In Search of Sugihara: The Elusive Japanese Diplomat Who Risked His Life to Rescue 10,000 Jews from the Holocaust* (New York: Free Press, 1996).

8. Yukiko Sugihara, *Visas for Life*, trans. Hiroki Sugihara and Anne Hoshiko Akabori (San Francisco: Edu-Comm Plus, 1995), 27.

9. Ibid.

10. Frank Shouldice, "An Irishman's Diary," *The Irish Times*, February 25, 2005, http://www.irishtimes.com/opinion/an-irishman-s-diary-1.418326.

Charles Dickens

1. Charles Dickens, *The Life of Our Lord, Written for His Children during the Years 1846 to 1849* (New York: Simon & Schuster, 1934), 17.

2. Ronan Deazley, *Rethinking Copyright: History, Theory, Language* (Cheltenham, UK: Edward Elgar Publishing, 2006), 95.

3. "The Press: Joseph's Son," *Time*, March 12, 1934.

4. Ibid.

5. Sir Henry F. Dickens, *Memories of My Father* (London: Victor Gollancz, 1928), 28–29.

6. John Forster, *The Life of Charles Dickens,* vol. 1 (Philadelphia: J. B. Lippincott & Company, 1872), 43.

7. Ibid., 57.

8. Ibid., 55.

9. David Macrae, *Amongst the Darkies and Other Papers* (Glasgow: John S. Marr & Sons, 1880), 127.

10. Maria Popova, "How to Be a Decent Person: Charles Dickens's Letter of Advice to His Youngest Son," Brain Pickings, accessed July 30, 2015, http://www.brainpickings.org/2013/02/07/charles-dickens-advice-to-son-plorn/.

11. Wolf Mankowitz, *Dickens of London* (London: Weidenfeld & Nicolson, 1976), 246.

12. John Forster, *The Life of Charles Dickens*, vol. 2 (London: Chapman & Hall, 1873), 300–01.

13. Macrae, *Amongst the Darkies*, 127.

John D. Rockefeller Sr.

1. Rockefeller Archive Center, Inglis interview, p. 1665, as quoted in Ron Chernow, *Titan: The Life of John D. Rockefeller, Sr.* (New York: Random House, 2004), 18.

2. Ida Tarbell, *History of the Standard Oil Company*, vol. 1 (New York: McClure, Phillips & Co., 1904), 40, as quoted in Chernow, *Titan*, 32.

3. Chernow, *Titan*, 10.

4. John T. Flynn, *God's Gold: The Story of Rockefeller and His Times* (New York: Harcourt and Brace, 1932), 401.

5. "Laura Spelman Rockefeller, 1839–1915," Rockefeller Archive Center, http://www.rockarch.org/bio/laura.php.

6. Andrew Robert Lee Cayton, *Ohio: The History of a People* (Columbus: The Ohio State University Press, 2002), 182.

7. "Laura Spelman Rockefeller," Rockefeller Archive Center.

Cristóbal Krusen is a screenwriter, film director, and author who has lived in Mexico, Australia, Belize, and the United States. In 1988, he founded Messenger Films, a nonprofit film production company. He studied English literature at Harvard University and also studied film and television at NYU and the Art Center College of Design. He most recently collaborated with Josh McDowell in the writing of Josh's memoir *Undaunted: One Man's Real-Life Journey from Unspeakable Memories to Unbelievable Grace*, which received a starred review from *Publishers Weekly*. He currently lives in St. Paul, Minnesota.

Connect with author

CRISTÓBAL KRUSEN

Cristobalkrusen.com

 @ CristobalKrusen

 cristobal.krusen

 linkedin.com/in/cristobalkrusen